MOTHER AMERICAN NIGHT

MOTHER AMERICAN NIGHT

MY LIFE IN CRAZY TIMES

JOHN PERRY BARLOW

with Robert Greenfield

CROWN ARCHETYPE
NEW YORK

All rights reserved.
Published in the United States by Crown Archetype,
an imprint of the Crown Publishing Group, a division of
Penguin Random House LLC, New York.
crownarchetype.com

Crown Archetype and colophon is a registered trademark of
Penguin Random House LLC.

Library of Congress Cataloging-in-Publication Data
Names: Barlow, John P. (John Perry) author. | Greenfield, Robert.
Title: Mother American Night : my life in crazy times / John Perry Barlow with
    Robert Greenfield.
Description: First edition. | New York : Crown Archetype, [2018]
Identifiers: LCCN 2017050430 (print) | LCCN 2017052223 (ebook) |
    ISBN 9781524760205 (e-book) | ISBN 9781524760182 (hardcover) |
    ISBN 9781524760199 (trade pbk.)
Subjects: LCSH: Barlow, John P. (John Perry) | Lyricists—United States—
    Biography. | Grateful Dead (Musical group)
Classification: LCC ML423.B256 (ebook) | LCC ML423.B256 A3 2018 (print) |
    DDC 782.42164092 [B]—dc23
LC record available at https://lccn.loc.gov/2017050430

ISBN 978-1-5247-6018-2
Ebook ISBN 978-1-5247-6020-5

PRINTED IN THE UNITED STATES OF AMERICA

Frontispiece photo by Elaine Barlow
Jacket design by Jessie Sayward Bright
Jacket photograph: Ted Wood

10 9 8 7 6 5 4 3 2 1

First Edition

For Willah Brave Barlow Dunwody, a vote of the future

CONTENTS

CONTENTS

The black-throated wind keeps on pouring in
With its words of a life where nothing is new.
Ah, Mother American Night, I'm lost from the light.
Ohhh, I'm drowning in you.

    —John Perry Barlow, "Black-Throated Wind"

Flight of the seabirds
Scattered like lost words.
Wheel to the storm and fly.

    —John Perry Barlow, "Cassidy"

We fray into the future, rarely wrought
Save in the tapestries of afterthought.

    —Richard Wilbur, "Year's End"

MOTHER AMERICAN NIGHT

NOT DEAD ENOUGH

I am determined to learn how to accept love, which I think may be the secret of life. If you can accept love, you can do damn near everything else. Giving love is easy and so most people go about thinking that they're fully capable in the love department because they can give it. But as I have learned, that is not the case, and how could it be? If you don't accept it, where are you going to get love to give?

My mentor in this regard is the only person I've ever met in my life who can seamlessly accept love: Gilberto Gil, the great musician and former minister of culture in Brazil. For him, it appears to be effortless. Since I would say that he is the most beloved person in the most loving country on the planet, it's very lucky for him and them that he can accept it so easily.

On April 16, 2015, Gil was performing at Davies Symphony Hall in San Francisco. On my way back from Huntsville, Texas, where I had been lured to give a speech, I spent hours tramping around the Atlanta airport in a brand-new pair of cowboy boots while waiting for a flight that would get me back home in time for Gil's show.

For years, I had been getting my boots from the Olathe boot company in Kansas. They were made of Norwegian elk leather, which is especially pliant and so could accommodate a bunion I have on my left foot that somebody once said should be in the Boone and Crockett big game trophy book of bunions if there had ever been one.

I already had about ten pairs of these boots that had been kept in walking condition by a wizard in San Francisco who said he could restore any cowboy boot that had ever been made, and, by golly, he could. But I had not been to see him for a while and in an act of desperation, I bought a pair of Norwegian elk boots from another company. Although they were not pliant, I said to myself, "How bad could they be during a short trip?"

Although I arrived in San Francisco too late to see him perform, Gil and I did then go back to the Mark Hopkins hotel, where the two of us sat up all night long talking in the lobby by ourselves. It was a rich moment, and an ironic one as well, because at the time, I had no idea whatsoever that I was about to embark on the greatest experience I could ever imagine in terms of teaching me how to accept love.

Having worn a gigantic hole in the index toe of my left foot by walking for hours through the Atlanta airport in those brand-new boots, I woke up the next morning, which also happened to be the twenty-first anniversary of the worst day of my life, with my right shoulder on fire. From past experience, I knew right away that I had contracted a staph infection in my blood and it had taken refuge in a major joint.

I went to Stanford Medical Center, where they said, "You're not running a fever, and since your white blood cell count is not elevated, we don't think you've got a staph infection. Take these pain killers and sleep aids and go home and see if it doesn't improve over a couple of days."

I went home. I took the pain killers. I went to sleep and when I woke up, all four of my major joints were on fire, both shoulders and both knees. I called my friend Dr. Beth Kaplan, who was then an emergency room physician at San Francisco General Hospital. She came down and checked me out and said, "You're dying. We've got to get you the fuck out of here." Which I then confirmed by puking up about a quart of blood.

They came and took me back to the Stanford Medical Center by ambulance. At Beth's insistence, they did this hideous thing called lavage where they opened up my joints and used a stream of antiseptics and antibiotics to clean out the infection. In the process, they also cleaned out all that was left of the cartilage in those joints.

They also installed a PICC line, which caused me to contract a second bacterial infection that set up camp in some hardware in my back. Suddenly, I couldn't walk. I was also not producing any red blood cells, and so they transferred me up to UCSF in San Francisco, where they stabilized my bone marrow.

While I was at UCSF, the doctor who had installed that hardware cleaned out the bacteria that had attacked it. I had no way of conveying to him that I was on an heroic amount of blood thinners to prevent a pulmonary embolism, and in the process, he created a hematoma that put a large blood clot about the size and shape of two golf balls between my spinal cord and the epidural sheath. They had to open me right back up at four o'clock in the morning to get it out of there. I had gone under the knife with him several times before, so I just had to be positive and trust him.

Before he did this, he said, "John Perry, I gotta tell you. I don't know what I'm going to find when I get in there, but I think unfortunately that there is a pretty good chance that I'm not going to be able to save any of your functions below T11." In other words, I would be paralyzed from my belly button down. I said, "You mean I'll never dance again?" And he said, "I'm not sure, but I think if you had one working eyelid, you'd still dance." Which remains one of the best compliments I've ever received.

So I went in there knowing there was a good chance that I was going to come out unable to walk again. When I woke up in the recovery room, my doctor was standing at the end of my bed and he said, "John Perry, move your toes." I did. And he started to cry. Because he had no idea if I was going to be able to do that and this was the only way to find out.

I was recovering from that when they decided they needed to be on the outlook for pulmonary embolisms, so they installed a filter in my vena cava to remove all the phlebitis-style clots from my blood-stream. In what I later learned was yet another iatrogenic failure, they displaced something that lodged itself in what had previously been my main coronary artery.

Later that evening, I was in the middle of an extremely stressful phone conversation with my business partner, who had been instru-mental in getting us the money for our pure water project, when I started feeling pain in my chest. I didn't know what to do about it at first and finally said, "I believe I've got to get off this call, I may be hav-ing a heart attack."

And in fact, the lower two ventricles of my heart had just stopped dead in their tracks and I had no heartbeat. So they hauled me off from the company of my daughter Leah and several other folks who had a pretty hard time taking in this spectacle. They took me to a side room and hit me with the paddles. Just like on TV. Nothing. They hit me again with the paddles with twice as much voltage. Nothing. Then they hit me the third time with so much energy that they burned my chest. But it still didn't start my heart.

Then an amazing thing happened. A young resident grabbed my arm, yanked me off the gurney, flung me to the floor, and jumped on my sternum with both of his knees. And my heart kind of went, "Well, if you're going to be like that about it, I guess I'll start beating again." It was like the cowboy heart reaction. "You *hit* me, you son of a bitch!"

If people code out for eight minutes like I did and then come back, they usually do so as a different person than the one who left. But I guess my brain doesn't use all that much oxygen because I appeared to be the same guy, at least from the inside. For eight minutes, however, I had not just been gratefully dead, I had been plain, flat out, ordinary dead. It was then I decided the time had finally come for me to begin working on my book. Looking for a ghost writer was not really the issue. At the time, my main concern was to not be a ghost before the book itself was done.

What amazed me most about this entire incident was that after so many years of thinking I really understood what happened when you died, I had not seen a goddamn thing. No upwardly sweeping rivers of light, no angels, no cherubim, no seraphim, no celestial beings. It all just went black. I'd gone down the tunnel of eternity and it had turned out to be nothing more than a cheap carnival ride to nowhere.

When I told my old friend and songwriting partner Bob Weir about this, he looked at me and said, "Well, it could be that you just weren't dead enough."

ONE

THE LITTLE RED BULL

Wyoming is a one-class state, and if you think you're better than someone else, they will tell you to your face that you're wrong. My mother, Miriam Jenkins Barlow, would have argued this point with you because, to the extent that there is aristocracy in that part of the world, she was kind of like Wyoming royalty.

Her great-uncle was a cattle baron named Amos Smith, who was the first human being to spend a winter in the high reaches of the upper Green River basin. Not even the Indians had ever tried to do that, but Amos had taken a bunch of cattle in there to graze because the grass was unbelievable. It started to snow early, and he got trapped.

I imagine it was a lot like what Hugh Glass, who was my hero when I was about seven years old, went through in *The Revenant*, with deep snow and lots of wind, but somehow he managed get through it. Having done that, Uncle Amos decided that the upper Green River basin, which was as fair as the garden of the lord and full of tall green grass for two or three months a year, would be wonderful for his cattle, because he could grow hay there and keep cattle year-round.

These were pioneering ideas, and so he hired a bunch of people to homestead for him on 160 acres of sagebrush with barely any water and nothing that you could raise because the entire growing season was about eighteen minutes long. I have actually seen it snow there on the Fourth of July. There's a joke in Pinedale about a stranger who comes to town shivering and asks one of the locals, "What do you people do around here in the summer?" And the local guy says, "Well, if it falls on a Sunday, we usually have a picnic."

Uncle Amos never had any children, but he did have three nieces, who were from Burlington Junction, Missouri, and one of them, Eva, married my grandfather Perry Wilson Jenkins, who was an astronomer and a mathematician and an incredible human being if not also terribly likable. Known to one and all as P.W., he had been born in Mount Carmel, Indiana, in 1867. His grandfather had served as an army officer during the American Revolution, and his father had fought in the Civil War. P.W. grew up on the family farm in Butler County, Ohio, and then attended Miami University in Oxford, where he was a member of Phi Beta Kappa and played quarterback on the football team.

P.W. went on to acquire multiple master's degrees in mathematics and geodesic engineering. By the time he was twenty-nine years old, P.W. became the youngest college president in the United States at Amity College in Iowa. While serving as a fellow at the University of Chicago in 1905, he was diagnosed with tuberculosis of the kidney, known back then as consumption. The doctor who removed one of P.W.'s kidneys didn't even bother to send him the bill because he figured the other kidney would kill P.W. before he could ever pay it.

P.W. was about thirty-eight years old when he came out west with Eva because he thought the mountain air might be good for him. He came with the expectation of dying quickly. But he didn't. Instead, he became quite a big deal.

First he went to a sanatorium in Colorado Springs and then to Wyoming, where he spent a couple of years working for Uncle Amos on his Mule Shoe Ranch, which turned out to be extremely salutary for him. When it looked like P.W. was going to live after all, Uncle Amos said, "Why don't you get a place of your own?" He grubstaked him a bit, and then P.W. bought a little homestead called the Westphall Place that was north of Cora.

It was soon called the Bar Cross Ranch; as a mathematician, P.W. had come up with a one-iron brand that was also a mathematical symbol and easy to apply. He then bought the Wright place, the Johnson place, and the Merschon place and started to accumulate a lot of adjacent land in the county.

When Uncle Amos died, he left all of his property to P.W.'s wife, Eva, and her two sisters. Her sisters were both farm girls back in Missouri and they immediately sold their shares to P.W. Pretty soon, he had bought himself a drugstore and a grocery as well as a stake in the State Bank of Big Piney, Wyoming. He also became a thirty-second degree Scottish Rite Mason and founded the Franklin Lodge in Pinedale.

In 1919, P.W. was elected to the first of his five terms in the Wyoming State House of Representatives, where he became Speaker pro-tem before going on to serve two terms in the state senate and as president. Because he didn't like to ride all the way over to Lander, the Fremont County seat, and because the line between it and Lincoln County ran right through the middle of his house, P.W. introduced the bill in the Wyoming State House of Representatives that led to the creation of Sublette County in 1923.

To the best of my knowledge, Sublette County, which comprises about five thousand square miles of land, is the only political jurisdiction that is based almost entirely on its watershed. P.W. did put the tiny town of Bondurant in it, but that was only so he could get enough votes from there to make Pinedale the county seat in a hotly contested election that was decided by just six votes.

P.W. named the county after William Sublette, a well-known mountain man who, along with his four brothers, trapped for the Rocky Mountain Fur Company. In the early nineteenth century people would come into Wyoming through South Pass, the only wagon route through the Rocky Mountains. In 1826, William Sublette blazed a shortcut between South Pass and the Bear River that became known as Sublette's Cutoff.

P.W. also tried running for governor twice, but that never worked out for him. The fact that he was quite unlikable had a lot to do with it. He was already in his mideighties when I was a kid, but my mother always felt that it was really important for me to learn whatever I could from him. So I would go out with him on long drives that let me see huge swathes of Sublette County. From the passenger seat I watched that old man take his 1954 Chevy Bel Air into places that I subsequently could not get to in a four-wheel drive.

I wouldn't say P.W. was ever loving to me in the conventional sense of the word, but I liked going out with him because he would address me as an adult and I would get to see things I would never have seen otherwise. And so getting to spend time with him as a kid gave me the opportunity to learn a lot of useful stuff about the adult world. My mother definitely felt that it was worth the risk of having us go out to some far distant place where P.W. might suddenly die behind the wheel, leaving me stuck there until someone else came along. Before we left the ranch, she would always say, "If Grandpa falls asleep for a very long time, that means he's gone. You don't go anywhere on your own. You just stay by the car." Fortunately for both of us, that never happened.

My mother herself always had a mixed relationship with her father. A big part of the problem was that while P.W.'s wife, Eva—my grandmother—was still alive, P.W. had already taken up with Girly Neal, who was like the scarlet woman of Big Piney, Wyoming. She was his secretary and traveling companion and about my mother's age, and my mother didn't care for this arrangement at all. Girly herself didn't help the situation much. Whenever she came down to Salt Lake City, Girly would stay with my mother at her sorority house at the University of Utah rather than at the house P.W. had there.

Around Pinedale, they called P.W. "the Little Red Bull." A bunch of different ranches ran a large cattle allotment in common, with the idea being that everyone would put out pure Hereford cattle that more or less matched. P.W. was a full-fledged member of the bull-buying committee, but he had his own goddamned ideas about this particular subject. He believed there was some significant virtue to crossing Hereford cows with Red Angus bulls, and so he bought a Red Angus and turned it out on the allotment. It was a rip-snorting little thing that tore up the turf and fucked everything in sight. That bull didn't look or think like any of the others, and in some respects it resembled P.W., who at five foot six was kind of diminutive physically.

Getting the little red bull kind of represented the way P.W. dealt with everything. Had someone else tried this, they would have gotten some shit for it, but with P.W. people were willing to say, "Well, he may know something about this," and so they let him do it. But I don't think anyone ever came up with a solid answer to the question of how they felt about either one of them, the bull or P.W. They all had mixed feelings.

Even though P.W. did amazing stuff for the area, including self-lessly laying in a lot of the ditch line and road line and creating the shape of the county, he wasn't the easiest person in the world to get along with. He knew he was a hell of a lot smarter than anyone around him in terms of raw intellectual horsepower, and so he was snappish. It was a character trait that became even more pronounced in my mother.

On June 19, 1955, when I was nine years old, P.W. wasn't feeling all that well and so he drove himself to the hospital, where he then died at the age of eighty-eight. He had outlived his doctor's diagnosis by fifty years.

TWO

NORMAN AND MIM

When my mother, Mim, was a freshman at the University of Wyoming in 1924, she was diagnosed with Pott's Disease, which was then called tuberculosis of the bones. She went to a quack doctor who had just gotten into the wonders of this new X-ray process, and he turned his X-ray beam on her hip for forty-five minutes.

The result was that she almost died of radiation sickness. She threw up for days, all of her hair fell out, and much of the skin on her hip was sloughed off. She was then informed that, regrettably, they had sterilized her. This was the Roaring Twenties, and my mother, who was a wild thing, believed she was now sterile, which made her even wilder when she recovered.

She kept a smoking-hot date book that included the night she met my father at the University of Utah in 1928. My mother was somewhat Victorian about it, but it was pretty clear that she and Norman just did it all night long. At various points in their lives, they both confessed to me that the reason they had stayed together for all those years was because they had never had better sex with anybody else.

Unlike my mother, my father was raised under oppressive Mormon circumstances. His father was a farmer in Bountiful, Utah, but the family didn't have a lot of money and they were always struggling. In the summertime, my father had to drive the family vegetable truck to the farmers market at four o'clock every morning.

Norman did, however, come from what amounted to Mormon royalty. On his side of the family, I have an ancestor I don't know how many times removed who signed the affidavit attesting to the reality of the golden tablets. That put my father pretty high up on the scale of credibility within the Mormon community. His entire family had been devout all the way down the line until my mother came along and snagged him.

By the time he graduated from the University of Utah in 1928, my father was not nearly so serious about being a Mormon. He still wanted to be regarded as a religious person but in the way that one is as a member of the burgher class. His goal in life was to become a banker.

Physically, my father didn't look much like me at all. He stood about six foot two and was well proportioned, a fine-looking man who could charm the scales off a chicken foot. He was also a great hand with the women. I would sit down with him and my mother for dinner in a restaurant and by the time we left, we would know all there was to know about the waitress.

My mother and father had an explosive connection that neither of them could exactly explain, and so when they decided to get married in 1929, my mother said, "All right, Norman, if you want to get married in the Mormon Temple for time and eternity, I'll do that." And he said, "No, I'd rather not." So they got married in the lobby of the Hotel Utah in Salt Lake City, right across the street from the temple.

With the beginning of the Depression, my father began to wonder about the wisdom of becoming a banker in Salt Lake City. Instead, he became the salvation of P.W., because my grandfather realized he was not smart enough about business to hold on to this large, kind of ungainly ranch he had assembled. And so P.W. happily turned the ranch over to my father.

For many years, my parents were kind of like the right-wing Wyoming version of John and Jackie Kennedy before they ever had kids, a glamorous couple who were both really attractive and well known for being able to have a real good time.

Then my father decided to run for state senate. During his first tour of duty in Cheyenne, he and Mim were having it off, as they were inclined to do, at the Plains Hotel, and it turned out that there was one egg left in my mother's ovaries. Much to her surprise and their mutual consternation, she got pregnant with me. At the time, she was forty-two years old. They had been fucking like minks for twenty years and had no expectations that this would ever happen.

She had to go to Jackson Hole to give birth because there was no hospital in Sublette County, and it turned out she was actually carrying twins, which they didn't know because this was in the days before ultrasound. When my identical twin brother looked out into the physical world on October 3, 1947, he decided that he was not interested and gave up right at the moment of birth. As I later learned, Elvis Presley's twin brother had done the same thing.

My mother never told me about any of this until I was about thirteen or fourteen. Other kids had imaginary friends who mysteriously disappeared as soon as they entered puberty, but mine stuck around. I never thought of him as having a name because he was too completely integrated into my life.

One day I said to my mother, "I feel this presence surrounding me all the time and it feels a lot like me. Do you have any idea what could cause that?" And she said, "I have an idea." She told me about my twin brother, and since then I've always been living for the two of us, which has made my own life immeasurably larger.

One of the best things about being an interruption in my parents' meteoric political career was that they both felt like I was this kid who had come to dinner and would leave just as mysteriously as I had arrived. So they spared me any set of expectations. They asked nothing of me and only ever disciplined me periodically.

My mother was incredibly cruel in a way, because she liked to make me her Little Lord Fauntleroy, which was unwelcome even when I was six years old. I was a boy in blue knee pants, and when she held bridge games with women of a certain age, she would put me on display. I would go around pouring Constant Comment tea for them all while making light conversation.

Although I was definitely the miracle child and the gift from God, both of my parents were raging narcissists, and so I was the miracle child because it suited their narcissism. But it did not suit their narcissism that there was now a third candidate vying for attention, and so they didn't always keep me around.

I never had a nanny, but I did have a bunch of broke-down alcoholic cowboys who were like nannies to me. They came and went, but some were long-term. There was a guy named Red Riniger who was a true cowboy and had an amusing way of approaching everything. Red was built out of beef jerky, and I spent an awful lot of time with him. There was a machine shop on the ranch because whenever anything broke down, we had to fix it. Red figured I would go down to the shop and start dicking around with stuff anyway, and so he taught me how to weld when I was four years old so I wouldn't blind myself. Most of our rolling stock was a lot older than me, and so we were constantly taking apart engines and repairing them because we couldn't afford to have someone come in from town to do it. When I got older, I turned out to be pretty good at it.

The ranch hands were all different than my mother and father, which was an asset as far as I was concerned. I once told my father I wanted to be a cowboy, and he said, "John Perry, a cowboy works for a salary. A cow man is someone who owns a ranch. *That* is what you want to be." And so I didn't learn how to brand cattle until the herd on the ranch was mine, and I formally became the cow man.

I like to say that I was raised largely by drunken cowboys and farm animals, and that is not as outrageous a statement as you might think. The Bar Cross was kind of a self-contained world, and it does take a ranch to fuck up a child.

THREE

HOME ON THE RANCH

Even before the Supreme Court made their decision in *Brown v. Board of Education* in 1954, my father thought that children everywhere should be going to integrated schools. He was nothing if not a fair-minded person. When I was five years old and about to start kindergarten, my father decided to introduce a bill in the state senate that would create an equal rights law in Wyoming.

Back then, the state's Democratic Party represented its white working-class people, and so Rudy Anselmi, the Democratic minority leader, said, "I don't know, Norm. In principle, I agree with your bill. But let's make this particular. We got this gal down there, this Negro lady who can't get a job because she's a Negro. Would you hire her to teach your son?"

And my father said, "It's amazing that you ask because I'm just setting up a school on the ranch for my son and some of the other kids who live there, and yeah, if she was qualified, I'd hire her." When my father met Juanita Simmons, he was impressed and hired her for the job. After that Rudy Anselmi enlisted everyone on his side of the aisle to support the bill, but it still took them five years to get it passed.

In 1952, there were no black people in Sublette County aside from Juanita and her husband, Jetty, who worked as a locomotive engineer in a switching yard. In the entire state of Wyoming, there were probably only somewhere between three and six hundred black people scattered along the Union Pacific railroad line. Juanita came to work as our teacher in an old schoolhouse at the Finn place that had two rooms. One was the classroom and Juanita lived in the other. Her husband, Jetty, would sometimes come up to stay with her but not as often as she or I would have preferred, because I thought this guy was God. Jetty drove Mallet locomotives, the biggest piece of rolling stock ever to hit the rails of the Union Pacific. Back then his job was kind of like being a rocket pilot. I thought he was coolest thing going.

For twenty days every other year, I went with my parents to Cheyenne while the state legislature was in session and attended school with a bunch of Catholic kids at St. Mary's, right next to the capitol. As the only Mormon there, I suffered a lot, mostly at the hands of the nuns. This was pre–Vatican II and my going to school there was always a weird little break in the rhythm of my life.

As a kid, I read like crazy. My parents bought me books, because it was fifteen miles to the public library in Pinedale. One thing that I read that was of pivotal importance was *The Book of Knowledge,* a twenty-volume encyclopedia for kids. I read every volume and that was fundamental for me, because it was my Internet. It really was. It introduced me to the idea that there were people out there who had gone to the trouble to find out how things worked and wanted to convey that information to others.

Although I was curious at the one-room schoolhouse, I wasn't a particularly good student. I was never worth a shit when it came to getting my homework done, and I'm still not. I also realized pretty early on that I could make a lot of headway on charm alone. But even that required some doing, because I was completely unsocialized at first. Whenever I got out among others who were my own age, I had virtually no social skills at all. I had to come up with a way to essentially reverse-engineer charm.

After I finished fifth grade, they closed down the little schoolhouse and started busing all the students into Pinedale. There were times when there was so much snow that the bus could not get into town, but we had snow planes, which had been cobbled together on skis with a big airplane engine on the rear that could really get up and going on a packed surface.

At home, things were not so great. My father was an alcoholic, but back then it was difficult to be someone of note in Wyoming politics if you weren't. He would go on binges sometimes, but he was never a mean drunk and not abusive in any way. He did make me angry and disappointed me a lot, though, in the way he took abuse from my mother that he didn't deserve and wouldn't have had to suffer if he hadn't been drinking.

My mother didn't like it. She also didn't like the fact that as my father got into politics, he became a bigger and bigger deal in Wyoming. At one point, my father was testing the waters to run for governor against Milward Simpson, whose son Alan later served as a U.S. senator from Wyoming. Milward and my father actually ended up flipping a coin to determine which one of them would be the next governor. I don't know if you could say my father won that coin flip or lost it, but Milward Simpson was the one who ran for the office and was elected governor in 1954.

While my father was now gallivanting around the state, he was pretty much fucking every woman he met. Women always know about these sorts of things, but my mother couldn't do anything about it except abuse the shit out of him. Then she went to see a psychiatrist in Denver who began giving her Dexedrine to cheer her up.

I was with her down in Denver when she had a calamitous nervous breakdown. I think I was about nine years old. She wound up in the same private sanatorium where Buffalo Bill had died. They were giving her electroshock therapy just about every week, so most of the time she didn't even have the slightest idea who I was. My father's older brother lived in Denver with his scrupulously Mormon family, and so I stayed with them.

I lived with them for about six months. It was easy for me because I took refuge in their Mormonism. I went to church with them and to Aaronic priesthood meetings, and every Wednesday night was family evening, when we would all pray together. I'd always had these kind of religious longings as a kid and had given away my entire allowance to Oral Roberts when I was in the second grade.

If you are going to be a real member of the Church of Jesus Christ of Latter-day Saints, I can tell you that they will have you doing something practically every second of the day. And that was actually a good thing. It made me feel like I was a part of something that was bigger than myself. The Mormon Church does not threaten you with hell because they don't have one. What they threaten you with—and they don't *really* threaten you—is this attitude of not understanding why you would ever want to leave the comfy bosom of your religious family.

When I went back to the ranch, I was still committed to Mormonism. Although my father did not feel that way, our foreman was a devout Mormon in spite of the fact that he had been struck by lightning three times. On the suffering and grace question, he really had a lot to say. He also had a very personal relationship with a very anthropomorphized God. As Voltaire once said, "If God has made us in his image, we have returned him the favor."

I was about eleven years old when my mother went upstairs and fired the twelve gauge. My dad was fooling around a fair amount by then and they'd had an argument that ended when she walked into the closet, grabbed the shotgun, and went upstairs. My father and I followed her, but she locked herself in one of the guest bedrooms and then *ker-blam!*

I will never forget the look that my father and I exchanged at that point. He broke down the door to get inside. She had fired both barrels into the ceiling and was sitting there with the smoking twelve gauge in her hand and this funny smile on her face, like she had finally gotten him to pay attention to her. It was a wildly melodramatic emotional act, a way for her to say "Hey!" that nobody could deny. It definitely left a mark on me.

Growing up on the ranch, I didn't have many friends my age, but there was a little girl named Gracie Alexander who lived up the creek about three miles away. She was nine and I was eleven, and we would ride to an abandoned homestead between her place and mine and pretend to be a frontier family. Gracie's father, Jack, was a cowboy and then a cow man who had gotten himself a little ranch. He had married a highly refined woman from the East who had come out to spend some time on a dude ranch in Wyoming and fallen in love with him. Back then, this sort of thing wasn't unusual—there were always a number of women who had come out and gotten themselves a cowboy for all the usual reasons. The mythology, primarily.

Maybe the marriage wasn't working out, but Jack had started drinking more and more, and he was really putting it away. His wife became concerned that this would be difficult for Gracie and so she invited her parents out from Providence, Rhode Island, to come and take Gracie back home with them. Gracie was the apple of her father's eye. For Jack, the sun rose and set around her. My best guess is that he found out about her mother's plan and just twisted off deep.

Back then, we were on a party line, and my mother was on the phone one day when someone picked up at the Alexander place and there was a lot of yelling. She couldn't make any of it out, and then there was a really loud sound that she thought was the screen door slamming or something. The phone stayed off the hook, and all you could hear was someone moving around in the kitchen on the other end.

What had happened was that Jack had shot Gracie's grandparents and her mother right away. He then went on living in the house for three days with Gracie and the family dog. Then he finished the job. He killed his daughter and shot the dog and then killed himself, too. Nobody went up there to check on them because it was the height of the mud season and difficult to get there.

Gracie was my closest friend, and I was devastated. I'm also pretty sure she watched her father kill her mother and grandparents. This was the first time I had ever lost anybody except for my grandfather, but death was something I became used to very early on. It's one of the leitmotifs of my life. I think everybody has a curriculum, and mine has always been women and death. These are two very challenging topics. It's not like I'm picking the easy horses, that's for sure.

FOUR

FOUNTAIN VALLEY

It actually took me quite a while to realize that I was just a hick in a hick town. The fact that most of the other kids were always rough on me had a lot to do with that. As far as they were concerned, I was the princely son of Norman and Mim Barlow, and many of them resented my parents for acting like they were the only exception to the one-class system in Sublette County.

The tough times started in elementary school in Pinedale, and then in middle school; a lot of physical shit went down as well. I wasn't getting beat up regularly but periodically. Once will suffice. When you find yourself in that kind of situation, you can turn yourself into a victim, and I actually became extremely de-socialized.

By then, I had seen James Dean in *Rebel Without a Cause* at the Skyline Theatre in Pinedale, which was a really special place. The upper part of the walls had a painted skyline with silhouettes of horses, cattle, teepees, trees, and all kinds of Western scenes, illuminated from behind by multicolored neon light that was so beautiful.

After I had seen *Rebel,* James Dean became the spirit that I modeled myself after. The movie had a huge effect on me. And it also turned out that I could actually comb my hair just like his.

I never did get to watch *American Bandstand* because we didn't have a television, but there was a rock 'n' roll radio station within range: XERF from Ciudad Acuña in Coahuila, Mexico, broadcasting over a 150,000-watt transmitter that made them sound like they were coming from some alien planet. I could pick up their signal on this little Sony transistor radio that my parents bought me in 1961 at the Seattle World's Fair.

A DJ called Wolfman Jack played music and aired ads for Don's Record Parlor in Eagle Pass, Texas, just across the border. Wolfman Jack was playing what in those days was still called race music. No one else I knew who was my age was listening to this stuff as avidly as I was. I was actually buying records from Don's Record Parlor. By the time I was fifteen, my friends and I would be driving around at night with the car radio set to Wolfman Jack, and we'd all be bumping and grinding to this music.

I finished my freshman year at Pinedale High School with a straight F average. A root vegetable could have done better. But I didn't give a fuck. I was in such a spiteful little mood back then that I was intentionally giving the wrong answer to questions both in the classroom and on tests.

By then, I already had a reputation. The very first thing I did on the day I turned thirteen and a half in 1961 was take my wages from the ranch and buy myself a little Honda motorcycle. Suddenly, I was free. I could go wherever I wanted whenever I wanted. Nobody could tell me what to do.

Almost immediately, I fell into a motorcycle gang, because all the other kids in my Boy Scout troop also got themselves little bikes. There were six of us, including a guy who later became the sheriff of Sublette County. We rode into this swampy area and built a clubhouse that you'd never guess was there until you were right on top of it. We would sit there and smoke Benson & Hedges cigarettes that I had stolen from my mother's freezer, where she would keep them around for guests. Back then, Benson & Hedges said quality, complete with a gold box.

We also undertook a lot of petty vandalism of which I'm not particularly proud. The motorcycles had been sold to us by an impassive, harmless gentleman named Herb Molyneux, a chainsaw salesman who had branched out into motorcycles. But he didn't offer us very good service, and at some point, we got cross-threaded with him. One night, we went into his place and raised hell with all the stuff he kept parked out back. Then we got into blowing up Coke machines. We found out that you could strategically place three M-80s inside a Coke machine in a way that would take out every single bottle in there as well as the coin mechanism. We weren't looking for money. We just wanted to fuck up the machines.

Over the course of time, we blew up every single Coke machine in town. Everybody knew we were the ones who were doing it, but they couldn't prove it and so there was no way for them to stop us. Finally, someone came and had a word with my father, who had just decided not to run for governor but was returning to his seat in the state senate. My father was told in no uncertain terms that if he wanted to go on holding that seat, it would be better for all concerned if he got his wayward son out of sight. And so we started looking for a school that was outside the sprawling confines of the great state of Wyoming.

The first school we picked was Suffield Academy in Connecticut, but they wouldn't let me in, which was completely understandable as I hadn't exactly had a distinguished academic career up to that point. We kept looking and found the Fountain Valley School in Colorado Springs, the go-to place for aristocratic kids from Wyoming who were also the sons of cattle barons. I was delighted to be going there, because I felt like I needed some kind of an upgrade in my life.

When I started at Fountain Valley, my parents flew us all there on the original Frontier Airlines, which was aptly named because it was truly a frontier experience. All their planes were DC-3s, a fantastic aircraft. I don't think any plane has ever exceeded the DC-3's safety record or capacity to take abuse and keep on flying. But it was a plodder. It had a service altitude of around sixteen thousand feet, which in mountainous terrain is kind of tricky, and flew so low over the mountains that you could actually count the antelope.

Frontier Airlines also had these really hard-bitten stewardesses. They weren't part of the larger aviation world, where stewardesses were sex symbols and there was a chance you might even be able to take one home. Because it was always cold in the plane, these stewardesses would come up and offer you an insulated foam cup filled with steaming hot bouillon. Whenever they gave it to you, you knew you were about to encounter severe turbulence. The bouillon was scalding hot and never cooled off until after it had ended up on your balls.

At Fountain Valley, Robert Hall Weir was rooming right across the hall from me. I met him in the first class I attended. I felt this presence behind me at my desk because the floor was shaking, and when I turned around, there was Weir with his foot just going *bang bang bang* against the floor. He had restless leg syndrome, which tends to attach itself to those with high math skills. In those days, he had reasonably short hair and a mono brow, and he wore these thick horn-rimmed glasses that gave him a look somewhere between genius and serial killer. He put out this vibe that I had a frequency setting for. It was not a vibe I had previously encountered, but it slotted right into something I had been looking for without even knowing it.

By then, Weir had already been bounced out of several private schools in California. He had a guitar, and we became fast friends because I loved listening to him play. I got him the Alan Lomax collection of American folk songs, and he learned them all. It was obvious to me that he was good at this and also that he wasn't much good at anything else.

Our bond was inflicted upon us by the shared experience of always being the goat. There was just something about the two of us that caused the other kids at Fountain Valley to give us merciless hell. I'd had some experience with this in Pinedale and was sort of prepared for it, but it was tougher to handle in a strange new environment because I was still just not good socially. Back then, I'd be hard-pressed to push two nouns against a verb in the presence of another human being.

Midway through the year, they finally figured out that Weir was dyslexic. Their response to this was to move him into a room with a guy who was *very* dyslexic. He was also the son of the CIA station chief in Saigon. Later he became a Green Beret and went off into Thailand like Colonel Kurtz in *Apocalypse Now* and recruited Hmong people for his own private army.

By the time they diagnosed his dyslexia, Weir was already acting out at every opportunity. At one point, the two of us flushed a lit M-80 down the toilet and raised hell with the plumbing. In biology class, Weir initiated a spitball fight, the spitballs being the internal organs of frogs.

That any of this was tolerated for even a second had a lot to do with the school itself. Back then, Fountain Valley specialized in admitting bright miscreants and was quite progressive. The school had been founded in 1929 on a large, beautiful ranch owned by a wealthy family in Colorado Springs. There was an architectural theme to the school, but the main thing was that we were all out there in the wide open spaces.

To say the least, the faculty was interesting. There was Mr. Kitsen, who had once water-skied in a tuxedo. I would not have been surprised to learn he had actually done that more than once. One of the English literature teachers was gay, and they somehow found out he had been buying gay material and canned him for that. Even then, I thought that was kind of cruel. We had a biology teacher we called Old Fartin' Martin Brown. He had once flown a tiny acrobatic airplane into one of those huge dirigible hangars at Moffett Field by Highway 101 south of San Francisco. As soon as he flew into the hanger, Martin Brown realized that the other door was closed and somehow managed to turn his plane around and fly back out.

The way Weir remembers it is that the school finally said that one of us had to leave. Since I certainly had not yet approximated my academic potential and had been a major behavioral problem, there was definitely some discussion about throwing us both out. But in the end the administrators decided to keep me.

After I learned that Weir had been kicked out of Fountain Valley, I wanted to spend more time with him so I convinced my father to hire him to work on the ranch that summer. My father had never seen anyone like Weir. Bobby would jump off his tractor while it was still running to try to catch a field mouse, and the tractor would end up in a ditch. He did that more than once.

Weir was there for forty or fifty days and loved it. We did stuff together that marked the beginning of full-on adolescence. I had this 1964 El Camino (still do) and we could make it to Pinedale, which was fifteen miles away, in ten minutes. Pinedale had a drive-in run by this hip guy in his twenties and his really hip girlfriend, and they had created a kind of country beatnik hangout, with lots of rockabilly on the jukebox. Weir would bring his guitar along, and the girls from Pinedale would be all over him. But Bobby was not yet the draw for women he later became. Back then he was a Christian Scientist who was saving himself for marriage. Part of him was still a good boy.

I eventually became so vexed at what I considered to be Fountain Valley's unfair treatment of Bobby Weir that I decided to go live with the Weir family in Atherton, California, where we would both attend this bizarre experimental school called Pacific High School. That year, the school project was making a submarine. Ambitious, right?

But at the last minute, I got a phone call from one of my summer school math teachers, a guy who had actually lived in the Haight-Ashbury before it became a big deal and was an aficionado of slant-six engines. He said, "You know, you've already cut and run once. Cut and run twice and you've got a pattern. And it's not a pattern that will serve you well." I could see the wisdom of that, so I went back to Fountain Valley. That decision was a real defining moment for me; after that I started to step up academically.

Fountain Valley had an associate dean named David Banks who had a lot of moral authority, and he basically explained Kierkegaard's categorical imperative to me so that I understood it: "What would the world be like if everyone behaved like you have? Is that a world you would wish to inhabit?" He applied that principle to running the school, and it had a hugely moderating effect on my behavior.

Weir and I did not see each other again for a long while, but we did write letters back in the days when people did that. I can still see his handwriting because he put little circles over all of his *i*'s, just like the girls would do. He wasn't effeminate. Just an artist, I guess.

FIVE

GETTING INTO COLLEGE

It took me about a year after Weir left school to get myself sorted out at Fountain Valley. By my senior year I had fine grades, but no real intention of going to college. Instead, I had this silly notion of becoming a knight of the open road. I was thinking of getting a truck driver's license, because there is something about driving long distances that creates a very fecund situation for me. The driving takes up just enough of my attention that it slows down the inhibitory factors creeping into my mind.

But one day I was talking to a friend back in Pinedale whose dad was on the draft board and he told me they were already salivating at the prospect that Little Lord Fauntleroy John Perry Barlow was going to somehow try to get out of the draft. They were going to classify me 1-A so fast that my head would spin, and then I'd be matriculating at the University of Saigon. That was the entire reason I decided to go to college.

I applied to five or six schools back east and took the summer to go look at them: Wesleyan, Trinity, Columbia, Yale, Brandeis, and Middlebury. I got the feel of all these places and figured that it was highly unlikely that more than one of them would want to admit me. It was also certainly possible that none of them would, which meant I would have to quickly come up with some kind of plan B.

To my stunned surprise, they all accepted me. What I didn't know back then was that a bell rang in every college admissions office whenever they got an application from someone in Wyoming. After I got all these acceptance letters, I was stumped. I didn't know quite what to do. So I took a big old silver coin and shuffled all the letters into two groups so I couldn't see them. Then I flipped the coin and eliminated three of them.

Yale, Columbia, and Wesleyan were left. I thought about it a lot. The thing with Columbia was that they started getting needy and sending me all of this stuff like I was a football star. They were putting the recruitment hustle on me, and something about that felt weird and made the place less attractive.

Then I started to think about all the people I knew who had gone to Yale, which was quite a few. There was a saying: "You can always tell a Harvard man but you can't tell him much." Yale was even more like that, except I didn't think these people were particularly smart. They all seemed kind of correct and dopey and I wasn't sure I wanted to be one of them. I didn't think New Haven was all that promising, either. It appeared about ready to go into something just this side of a race war.

At the end of this somewhat weird process, Wesleyan emerged as the one. And God, I am glad that it did, because my time there had a great deal to do with who I became and made it possible for me to be successful in five or six different fields.

Before leaving Fountain Valley, I used the occasion of my graduation party to break into the headquarters of NORAD, the North American Air Defense Command. Had we all been drinking that night? Oh my God, yes. During my last semester at Fountain Valley, 25 percent of my class got themselves kicked out of school for drinking. Not beer. Distilled spirits like vodka and gin were far more highly favored because they always came on strong.

The party itself was on a ranch that belonged to the family of one of our students, situated right at the base of Cheyenne Mountain. It wasn't a particularly long walk from there to NORAD, but without having intended to do so, we somehow managed to circumvent all the guard posts. The front door itself was unguarded, and so we walked right into the headquarters.

Eventually, someone noticed us and called the guys with the chrome-plated helmets and sky-blue uniforms. These special MPs hustled us the hell out of there as quickly as they could, but they didn't actually punish us. I think they just didn't want anyone to know that a bunch of drunk high school kids had walked right into NORAD.

The larger point here is that until I was forty years old, I assumed that at some point during my lifetime, somebody would let a nuclear missile fly and then they would all launch and the world as we knew it would go up in smoke in a mushroom-shaped cloud. Because of NORAD, a high percentage of those ICBMs would have been headed right to where I was going to school. So it certainly looked to me like there was a good chance that we all might die long before we got old.

As a kid, when I had to go to school part-time in Cheyenne because the state legislature was there, we did frequent duck-and-cover drills. Many of the first major ICBMs, the really big ones that they still use to put stuff in space, were based at the Francis E. Warren Air Force Base right outside Cheyenne, which made it another prime target for nuclear destruction. I'll never forget being in a room on the fifth floor of the Plains Hotel in Cheyenne when I heard a commotion. I looked out the window and coming down the street was an Atlas missile. It was fucking huge, almost as long as the block itself. I can't describe how I felt about that. A part of me was still the excited twelve-year-old who had been a member of the science-fiction book club. On one level, actually seeing that Atlas missile was the apotheosis of my dreams.

Yet, on another level, it also embedded into my consciousness forevermore the very real threat of imminent nuclear annihilation. Every single one of us who grew up back then has this scar that is so pervasive we hardly even know it's there. It gave my entire generation a soupçon of pure nihilism.

SIX

WESLEYAN

At Wesleyan, I was a total fish out of water. Just about everybody who had been admitted there before me was a really smart Jewish kid from Scarsdale, which I definitely was not. My class was different, because Wesleyan's new director of admissions had just arrived with a fierce vision to diversify the student body and admit fewer well-scrubbed, well-rounded, well-mannered white boys.

He went looking for extreme students of all kinds. People with the novelty gene. He was looking for trouble, which in the end was what he damn well got. The freshman class he admitted was 12 percent black, and these were not suburban blacks. They were black kids from little towns in the south and the inner city. They were all just as baffled to be there as I was and, as a consequence, constituted a large percentage of my first friends.

At the time, Wesleyan was small, isolated, and still an all-male college, which sent us on constant visits to women's colleges such as Smith and Mount Holyoke and Sarah Lawrence in search of female companionship. In fact, I often say that in college, I majored in back-country motorcycle tours of New England. I also always tended to keep some kind of relationship going with a student at Sarah Lawrence so I could attend Joseph Campbell's lecture every Monday morning.

There was a fraternity system at Wesleyan, and I got into Alpha Delta Phi straight away. The Wesleyan chapter was not at all like the one at Dartmouth that became the inspiration for *Animal House*. Nothing could have been like that one, because they truly were completely off the hook. I went up there once for Winter Carnival weekend and saw a guy squatting over the punch bowl and actually taking a crap. Even back then this was outside behavior. Nothing like that happened in our chapter, because we were the literary house on campus. The most scandalous event to occur in public view was when the poet Charles Olson insulted Richard Wilbur, who at the time was the poet laureate of the United States.

By far, the faculty member at Wesleyan who was the biggest influence on me was provost Willie Kerr, the well-known historian and the closest thing I've ever met to a saint. Willie was a wonderful, wonderful man. He always had a little group of students and alumni gathered around him that I was really honored to become a part of.

In the best sense of the term, Willie was the most Christian man I had ever met, and he was a continuous light in terms of his moral clarity. We would go out with him to the apple orchards of central Connecticut in his '49 Mercedes convertible and have picnics where we would resolve not to talk about people but rather ideas.

At the time, Wesleyan had an academic press that among other things produced *My Weekly Reader,* the publication that every student in America read back then. It helped shape the consciousness of my generation. Wesleyan sold the press to Xerox for stock in 1965, and the value of that stock just kept right on increasing until it blew everybody out of the water. The result was that Wesleyan eventually became by a large margin the richest academic institution per capita on the planet. They spent money lavishly to bring in guest lecturers such as John Cage, Stephen Spender, and Jerzy Kosinski.

I spent a lot of time with Kosinski, a truly deeply wild human being who would try goddamn near anything. When Kosinski first came to the United States, he had a job in a parking garage in New York City. With the full consent of his customers, he would yank the relatively old engines out of their Porsches and replace them with brand-new ones, a service for which he would then be paid handsomely in cash.

Paul Horgan, the novelist who won two Pulitzer Prizes for History, was influential on me in another way. He was the one who integrated me into the Center for Advanced Studies, another artifact of Wesleyan's newfound wealth, intended to foster an environment where unique thinkers could interact with students and one another in order to come up with completely new ideas. Horgan was a provincial gentleman from Albuquerque, as well as a man of great polish. He took me under his wing and guided me and while I didn't always go through the straits and narrows by following his advice, it was always pretty clear to me what a gentleman would do in certain circumstances based on what he would have done.

Shortly after I arrived at Wesleyan in the fall of 1965 I went to a mixer at Vassar College. A dapper Indian fellow was hitting on all the girls and seemed to be quite a hit himself. I asked him where he was from, and he said he was staying at a place not too far away. I asked where and he said, "Oh, in Millbrook." Then he asked if he could get a ride back there. So I took him home after the mixer was over and the next thing I knew, I was at the Castalia Foundation, which was what Timothy Leary was then calling the group of people who were living communally with him and taking LSD together.

At that time, the scene at Millbrook was just getting started. The place itself was incredible, a huge estate with massive iron gates and a long driveway that led up to a white four-floor mansion with God only knows how many rooms. We showed up there at one-thirty in the morning, and the place was jumping. I was seventeen years old and thinking, *Holy shit! This is a new part of reality that I've not yet experienced.* Music was playing and people were walking around, some of them high on acid. I knew nothing about that, and I didn't know anything about any of these people. I just thought, *This scene definitely bears further observation.*

I've remembered going to Millbrook for the first time so many times over the years that it has become coated with a gazillion layers of memory, and so there is no way in the world that I can see it clearly now. What I did know for certain is that something incredibly significant was happening to me when I drove up to the main house. I knew I was at one of those crossroads in my life where everything would be different after that. I didn't know why back then, and I still don't.

At Millbrook, Tim Leary was obviously the guy with the mojo. He looked older than he actually was, but that didn't matter because in every respect, he was the alpha male. The alpha males I'd known back in Wyoming were all very macho and had a quiet certainty like Gary Cooper or Jimmy Stewart, but I thought Tim was sort of pesky. Everything he said or did contained a secret trap. He would seem to be going along with you and then he would ambush you with something you had said that you did not see coming, completely changing the nature of the discourse to your disadvantage.

This was a whole new version of the alpha male, because it was also based on Tim's understanding of women. He made being charming an end unto itself, and his charm was usually directed at members of the opposite sex. It also had a distinctly theatrical quality, and much of that was also a goal unto itself.

I hung out at Millbrook for a while and then drove back to Middletown. I then learned that some of my fellow students at Wesleyan had already taken acid, and that there were also folks there who had been involved with Leary during his previous incarnation as the director of the Harvard Psilocybin Project, including David McClelland and David and Sara Winter. They got me interested in a report about the Good Friday Experiment, which Walter Pahnke and Leary had conducted at Boston University's Marsh Chapel in 1962 to determine whether ingesting psilocybin could help induce subjects to have a religious experience.

All that really hit home with me, because I was a formerly religious kid who had fallen from grace. I wanted more than anything to return to a sense of belief, and the idea that I could take something that would do that for me appealed to my American sense of engineering. I was all over the idea, because it seemed to me that I could pull a lever or yank a chain and somehow deliver the mechanical into the spiritual.

In the spring of 1965, I took LSD for the first time in a fairly controlled setting at Wesleyan. In a sense, there is only one real trip, the first one. After that, you are only confirming what has already been revealed to you. I've probably taken psychedelic substances of one kind or another more than a thousand times, but my sense of the universe was changed forever the first time I took LSD. From then on, I was permanently rewired.

My first trip was all positive though a little scary, but I was somebody who had always worked on scaring himself. Wesleyan had a distinguished world music program that brought in people such as Ravi Shankar and Ali Akbar Khan and others of that caliber. Every Friday evening, there would be a concert and a curry dinner in a converted farmhouse outside of Middletown. Before the concert began one Friday night, a friend whom I had always regarded as a darkly magical character handed me a capsule of LSD. I took it when Ali Akbar Khan started playing, and I sat down to listen to the music. About half an hour later, I could literally feel the music on my skin. Then I could taste and smell it as well. All my senses were fusing into one. I also had the strong perception that with every beat of the tabla, a splash of what I now know to be fractal webbing would leap from that area of the room and sparkle across all the walls.

Seeing and feeling those fractals in the music, I experienced the complete connectedness of everything. At that moment, I knew for the first time that I was experiencing things as they really were, which is utterly continuous. There was not one thing and another thing. It was all the same thing, the Holy Thing.

The Holy Thing I experienced that night didn't seem to be related to a God that was actually only a greatly enhanced version of someone like me. Rather, it seemed to me that God was the universe and we were God and that it was all God and that everything was holy.

I had taken a significant dose and couldn't speak when the concert ended. A couple of my friends took me back to where I was staying. We

39

lit some candles, put on some music, and sat there listening all night long without attempting to say very much. For the first time in my life, I seemed able to let everything go through my mind without straining the system. I went someplace overwhelmingly different that night and, to a large extent, I have stayed there throughout the rest of my life.

I subsequently had trips where that same kind of opening felt terrifying. On those occasions, I couldn't sustain enough conventional reality to feel that I was still myself. Instead, my self had become so fragmented that its bits and pieces seemed like they would never reassemble into something that was recognizably me. But I learned how to be grateful for those horrors as well, in that they helped me understand the fragile miracle of my own being.

Another thing that happened to me that night was that I began believing again that the universe had a purpose and was in fact working fine. Not that the meaning or direction or shape of that purpose could ever be understood by anyone, but that it is possible to have faith in it without knowing any of those things.

With the possible exception of having children, taking that trip was the most important thing I have ever done. In terms of creating the person I am now and how I approach the world, why I do what I do, and what I think it's all about, no other experience in my life has been so transforming.

It certainly changed the focus of my intellectual interests. Up to that point at Wesleyan, I had been preparing myself to major in physics. Suddenly my focus was oriented much more toward religion, especially the Eastern philosophical traditions that seemed to describe the insights that I had been given that night. I began reading mystical literature from other traditions, including such seers as Meister Eckhart, Saint John of the Cross, and Saint Teresa of Ávila. By doing so, I learned that it was possible within the Western tradition to engage in mysticism, which was generally held in low regard in our culture.

I also subscribed to the *Psychedelic Review* and got into it all in a very academic way. After reading what Gordon Wasson, Aldous Huxley, and J. B. S. Haldane had written about psychedelics, I switched my major from physics to comparative religion. I was thinking that what I really wanted to be was some kind of new minister without portfolio, a seeker for spiritual experience.

Millbrook itself became like Byzantium to me. We were the Eastern Orthodox religion, and I had visited Byzantium once in a dream and created this huge castle of my own devising around it. Although I didn't return to that scene for a long time, there was this other thing on the West Coast that was going on that, in my Eastern Orthodox way, I regarded as the ultimate heresy. Which was Ken Kesey, the Merry Pranksters, and the Grateful Dead.

SEVEN

GOOD OLD GRATEFUL DEAD

To my great surprise, I found out that my best friend, Bob Weir, from whom I had been disconnected for years, was now a member of the house band of the Western apostasy. One of the straightest guys from Fountain Valley, who was serving as a lieutenant JG in the U.S. Navy, wrote me a letter and said, "I don't know if you know this, but your friend Bobby Weir has resurfaced and he's part of this whole shebang."

In June 1967, the Grateful Dead were going to play their first East Coast gig at the Café au Go Go in New York City, so I went down there to see them and reconnect with Weir. This was also when the Six-Day War broke out in the Middle East and *Sgt. Pepper's Lonely Hearts Club Band* was released in America. It was a week of great potency, and for me personally it was a very good week to be Zelig.

The first time I saw the Grateful Dead perform, they were playing through Fender Princeton amps in a basement with brick walls in Greenwich Village. I got what they were doing right away. I also got to reconnect with my erstwhile official best friend, Weir, who had been off doing Acid Tests for a while, none of which he had seemed to have completed. His hair was down to his waist, and he had the thousand-yard stare to the max. He was way the fuck out there. He could see all the way to the other end of the cosmos and didn't have much to say.

I had never met any of the Dead before, but that night I talked a lot with Phil Lesh, whose eloquent and wide-ranging interests impressed me enormously. I actually felt a great deal more immediate compatibility with him than with Weir, who now seemed utterly different to me. I very much wanted to create a relationship with the Dead, but I didn't know how to go about it. So I began thinking, *What can I do for these guys to demonstrate my own mojo so I can be part of their thing?*

After the show that night, Weir and I walked around the Village trying to catch up on things. We were sitting underneath the arch in Washington Square at about four-thirty in the morning when this pale green Ford Falcon pulled up, and it was like a thousand clowns got out of the car. Kids from Long Island. Bad kids. About ten of them.

They immediately surrounded us and started dancing around yelling, "Kill the pig! Drink his blood!" Obviously they intended to beat the crap out of us. Weir looked up at them and said, "I sense violence. And you know whenever I feel violence in myself, there's a song I sing that has always had a calming effect on me. Let me see if you would like to sing it with me."

These kids were completely blown away. Suddenly, Weir had gone meta on them. This was not a concept on Long Island. He started singing "Hare Krishna," and they were actually singing it with him, and I was thinking, *Jesus, do you suppose this might work?* I was singing along literally like my life depended on it. Then, at a certain point, one of the guys went, "Fuck this!" He gave the signal and they went right ahead and beat the crap out of us.

Although I still considered what the Dead were doing to be heresy, I wanted to give them something, so I said, "Look, I happen to know where Timothy Leary lives. How would you like to go up there and see him?"

On the sparkling June morning that I drove the Dead up to Millbrook, I stopped by my favorite record store on West Sixth Street in Greenwich Village and picked up *Sgt. Pepper's Lonely Hearts Club Band.* I had heard it the night before during intermission at Café au Go Go, and I was thinking, "The Dead are pretty great but Jesus Christ, if you want to hear LSD music, this is it."

I also picked up Phil Lesh and his amazing date for the weekend, a girl known as Essra Mohawk, whose real name was Sandy Hurvitz. She was a musician who had appeared with the Mothers of Invention and been given the nickname "Uncle Meat" by a member of the band, which was how Frank Zappa would then always introduce her to the audience. She had a smart little mouth on her and was terrific.

My girlfriend, who at the time was going to Bard, was with me. She had been with Bobby and me the night before when we got the shit kicked out of us. I was in such bad shape that she was concerned about my ability to drive, but it was just a beautiful day, and the Taconic State Parkway was never more glorious.

So it was the four of us and Weir and his beautiful, quirky French girlfriend in my car and news was pouring in on the radio about the Six-Day War in the Middle East. I hadn't been to Millbrook in nearly a year but the guy at the gate recognized me so I just drove right up to the main house and said, "These are my friends, the Grateful Dead." And they said, "Fine."

The most significant aspect of our visit was not my offering of the Dead but that I had brought up *Sgt. Pepper's.* They had not yet heard the album at Millbrook, and so there was a big ritualistic ceremony to listening. It was one of those sixties scenes where there was a lot of cheap printed Indian cotton around and brass lamps and the smell of incense and patchouli oil and cat piss. After the record was over, Tim Leary stood up and in this incredibly pretentious, sententious mystical voice, said, "My work is finished. Now it's out." In a funny way, he was right. Because from that point forward, it was all going to take care of itself.

We all stayed there for several nights, and it was a total collision of two different worlds. At Millbrook, they were still doing the Indian thing and sitting meditation, and the Dead looked at it like, "What is this horseshit?" They had a fine nose for that sort of thing and saw right through it all real fast. Now I saw through it as well, and I was a little embarrassed that I had brought them there.

Mountain Girl had come up with Jerry and the rest of the band separately, and the real point of contact between the Eastern Orthodox and the Western apostasy was when she and Tim talked. In her way, she was quizzing him. Back then, she always interrogated everyone. Mountain Girl was running the dozens on Tim, and he pretty much passed the test. She thought he was a little vague and slipping and sliding, and in those days, Mountain Girl was really hard on slipping and sliding. She has always had an extremely keen nose for bullshit and was a lot tougher on it then than she is now.

I distinctly remember telling Tim about the beating that Weir and I had received in Washington Square Park the night before. We were in the kitchen in Millbrook, and he kept shaking his head in this completely phony, caring way. It was total bullshit and I knew it. It was sort of incumbent on him to tsk-tsk and he was doing a great job of it, but I knew better. I knew he didn't really give a damn.

Leary had no idea what it was like to get beaten up in Washington Square at four-thirty in the morning. He kept trying to understand what I was saying, but his persona was coming up with, "Why must there be this violence among us? Why can we not rise above these base things?" It was just complete horseshit, and it really did put me off him.

What Millbrook had been for me before was something different from what it now seemed to be. The whole scene was a big disappointment. I saw it all as pretentious and self-serving and basically exploitive. Everyone there was really getting off on the fact that they were hip enough to be using a substance that had the power to irrevocably alter the human brain.

Everyone at Millbrook was in the "prana receptive state" echo chamber, and the Grateful Dead were out to kick ass and have fun. They recognized one another as members of related but entirely different tribes. Unlike the people who lived at Millbrook with Tim Leary, the Dead were saying, "Katy, bar the door. Let's kick the television.

Let's really kick the shit out of the television! Let's turn the television into a refrigerator and see if that works." After that day I turned my back on the Eastern Orthodoxy and began doing my own thing in the Western apostasy, and I had nothing more to do with Tim Leary for years.

EIGHT

SUMMER OF LOVE

I didn't know all that much about what was going on in San Francisco until I got out there in June 1967. I stayed on and off in the Grateful Dead house at 710 Ashbury, and it was a weird scene indeed. By then, various people had gotten so far out on the edge that if they had gone any further, they would have been institutionalized.

All of it both repelled and attracted me, but I was really put off by the scene on Haight Street. Whenever I walked down Haight during the so-called Summer of Love, I was accosted by hostile, wild-eyed young men saying, "Grass, acid, speed? Grass, acid, speed?" I would rather have dealt with insurance salesmen. These guys had no money and were so stoned that they didn't care; people were eating dog food straight out of the can.

By 1967, the flag saying "Come here and do whatever you fucking well please" had been up long enough that everyone who was inclined to do so had showed up. In many cases, they were the last people in the world that you would have wanted to see doing so. The Gray Line buses had already started making regular trips down Haight Street so all the tourists could look at the freaks. The Dead had this big Red Chinese flag at 710 Ashbury, and one day Weir, who was then in another universe, got naked, grabbed the flag, and ran down the street alongside the bus. He gave them a show. There were a lot of people who were inclined to do that in order to say, "You came to the zoo. Here's one of the animals exhibiting native behavior."

Bobby had set up camp on a pestilential brown couch on the second floor of the Dead house. The room had once been a library but was now home to the stereo and a huge collection of communally abused records. He had a paper bag at the end of the couch in which he kept most of his worldly possessions.

Bobby was always the kid in the band and because I was the kid's kid, I took a fair amount of shit from everybody. The Dead were always very hard on Bobby, like the kids at Fountain Valley had been. We had both thought it was going to be a whole new deal for us after school, but no, here it was all over again. So we were bonded by that as well.

In the house at 710 Ashbury, Jerry Garcia was definitely at the center of the scene, and my interactions with him were always somewhat uneasy. When I first got together with the Dead in New York, Garcia had wanted to ride out to the Guild guitar factory in Westerly, Rhode Island. He knew the son of the guy who owned the company and wanted to take the tour and get specs on guitars. We all rode out there in my car.

He and Mountain Girl were in the back seat, and she was pretty hot in those days. At one point, I looked up into the rearview mirror and found Mountain Girl staring back at me with a distinctly salacious look. This look was intercepted by Garcia, and he went into a black mood. He didn't say anything about it at the time, but he gave her three kinds of hell about it later on. From that point on, Garcia always treated me poorly because he thought I was trying to steal his girlfriend, and so he became immediately unknowable to me.

During that summer, I met Augustus Owsley Stanley III for the first time. The Dead house at 710 Ashbury was far too funky for Phil Lesh, the professor, so he kept a separate place up the street. He lived there with this incredibly beautiful girl named Florence Nathan, now known as Rosie McGee, who was always wandering around naked. I'd come by and there'd be Florence with no clothes on. She'd say, "Phil's not here right now." And I'd say, "Tell him I came by." She'd say, "He'll be back." I'd say, "Well, all right . . . I'll wait," and then we'd sit around and talk.

I was up there one day when this feverish little man came in. He was clearly older than me but somehow seemed ageless. He was wearing a blazer with brass buttons on it and I said, "That looks like it needs a pocket patch. You need a coat of arms. A family crest. Some damn thing." And he said, "You know, I was thinking exactly the same thing at this very moment! And here's what I was thinking. I was thinking about a big *O* made out of flame wrapping itself through the indole ring." Luckily for me, I just happened to know that the indole ring was a six-membered benzene ring fused to a five-membered ring containing nitrogen that was found in psilocybin and LSD.

"Right?" he said. "Through the indole ring and radiating in various directions. What would you think of that?"

"That sounds pretty good," I said. "Is one of your initials *O*?"

"I'm Owsley," he said.

"So far that doesn't mean a great deal to me," I said, "but it looks to me like it's about to."

Owsley, whom everyone called Bear, was around all the time that summer. I got a lot of acid directly from him during this period, and all of it was very good because it was so clean. However, his personal trip with everybody was adversarial. I was not a rival, but he did see me as a good sparring partner. I don't know if he would have said that I was as smart as him, but he might have said that I came closer than most.

The most dominant memory I have of the Dead performing that summer was when they played the American Legion Hall on the south shore of Lake Tahoe. Weir got so excited that he threw the microphone stand off the stage. Not on purpose. It was all just part of him finding himself. At one point after that show, I ended up with Bobby in a Land Rover full of tools and two girls whom we were trying to get to do it with us in the cold, gray dawn in a forest clearing. It was a nadir.

After we got done with that, I had to drive the Grateful Dead truck back to San Francisco because the band was flying to Toronto to perform with the Jefferson Airplane. I asked Bear if he had anything that would help me stay awake behind the wheel, and he handed me something that turned out to be STP, a psychedelic substance first synthesized by Alexander Shulgin. STP supposedly stood for "Serenity, Tranquillity, and Peace," but I had never heard about this stuff before. I thought it was just some kind of upper.

What I came to realize was that coming on to this drug completely unprepared was a major mistake. I somehow got back to the city, but as I began driving across the Oakland Bay Bridge, the bridge and I were both breathing violently. After I managed to get to the other end, I pulled over, parked the truck on Fell Street, and walked back to the Dead house.

That Bear himself hadn't given me a heads-up as to what I would experience on STP was just the way he was. Insofar as Owsley was concerned, there was a right way and a wrong way to do everything. If you did anything in any way but his, you were pretty much an idiot. But if you wanted to be an idiot, that was up to you and he wouldn't be surprised that you chose to do so. He even had it down to where if you smoked dope in anything but Chantecler rolling papers, you were an idiot because he had analyzed them all. What made it worse was that you knew he had, and that he was probably right. He had put far more energy into it than I would have ever wanted anybody else to do, so I had to go with it. I began paying careful attention to all of his many pronouncements.

I also met Neal Cassady that summer. On nearly a nightly basis, Neal would hold court in the tiny kitchen at 710 Ashbury. He would carry on five different conversations at once and still devote one channel to talking to people who weren't there and another to the kind of sound effects made when the human cranium explodes, or that ring gears make when they disintegrate.

As far as I could tell, Neal never slept. He would toss back Mexican Dexedrine green hearts by the shot-sized bottle and grin and cackle while jamming on into the night. Despite such behavior, he seemed at the ripe old age of forty-one to be a paragon of robust health. With a face out of a recruiting poster and a torso, usually raw, by Michelangelo, he didn't seem quite mortal to me.

Neal and Bobby were perfectly contrapuntal. As Cassady rattled on incessantly in the kitchen of the Dead house, Bobby would just stand there completely mute while spending hours preparing his macrobiotic diet and then chewing each bite no less than forty times. While Neal talked, Bobby just chewed and listened.

Whenever Neal got really high and was flying on Dexedrine, he would take off his shirt, put on a pair of headphones so he could listen to a jazz record on the stereo, and begin juggling a forty-ounce ball-peen hammer in the air while singing scat. Bobby would lay there on the couch watching with his eyes wide open, and it seemed to both of us that what we were seeing could not be real. It was like Neal had become a vision that Bobby was creating.

I have a vague recollection of driving someplace one night in San Francisco with Neal and an amazingly lascivious redhead. The car was a large convertible, quite possibly a Cadillac, made in America back when we still made cars out of solid steel, but its bulk didn't seem like nearly enough armor against a world that kept coming at me so fast and close. Nevertheless, I took comfort in the thought that, having lived this way for so long, Neal Cassady was probably invulnerable. And if that were so, then I was also within the aura of his mysterious protection.

As it turned out, I was wrong about that. About five months later, just four days short of his forty-second birthday, Neal was found dead next to a railroad track outside San Miguel de Allende, Mexico. He had wandered out there in an altered state and died of exposure in the high desert night. Exposure seemed right to me. He had lived an exposed life. By then, it was beginning to feel like we all had.

NINE

HARVARD YARD

Although I knew I hadn't been in San Francisco for the pinnacle of the magic, that was okay with me. I tripped while I was around the Dead and went to the Fillmore and spent time in Golden Gate Park. I didn't take acid with Weir that summer. To the best of my knowledge, I have never taken acid with Weir. He doesn't actually like the stuff. It's not his drug.

Nonetheless, by the time I got back to Wesleyan in the fall, I was pretty crazy. I didn't chill out in San Francisco or get some vision of peace, love, and flowers. Instead, I decided to become a suicide bomber. If you put it into the context of those times, I think everybody I knew then was completely freaked out, each in his own individual way.

As a freshman, I had helped organize the Students for a Democratic Society chapter on campus. The following year, I became the first sophomore to ever be elected to the College Body Committee, a five-man student governing board much like the Politburo in the Soviet Union. As a senior, I ran for student body president.

I represented the anti-jock faction at the school. There were about seventeen candidates on the ballot, and the jocks were so fucking stupid that they thought if they listed me as number seventeen on their ballots, I would stand no chance whatsoever of winning the race. Thanks to them, when the voting ended, it turned out I had fulfilled the necessary requirements to be elected.

This was a time when everyone was big on participatory democracy, and during the next year, a group formed with the goal of completely changing the system of student government, which was not terribly representative at the time because it involved only the five members of that student governing board. So the group decided to try putting together a student legislative body and a constitution.

I kept trying to help them with this process, but they didn't want my assistance. Meanwhile, the other students on the College Body Committee all graduated during the course of the summer, leaving me as the only member. That was when I became the de facto student body president, because everyone on campus was waiting for this spiffy new student-government constitution to be created. Actually, I became the de facto dictator of the student body.

As part of my duties, I was in charge of $600,000 of student funds. There was a group of black students on campus called the Ujamaa Society, which had formed in opposition to the Black Panthers, who were serious as shit even within themselves. In any case, the Ujamaa Society published an open letter in the *Wesleyan Argus*, the student newspaper, saying that if I didn't turn over half of the student funds to them as reparations for slavery, they would kill me.

I knew a lot of these guys because they had been my friends when I first came to Wesleyan. So I went over to the Ujamaa Society shortly before their house (which had previously been where the president of the school lived) burned down and I said, "Guys, this is nuts. You're not going to kill me."

And one of them said, "We just want to kill what you represent."

I said, "*I* want to kill what I represent. If you can help me kill that, it would be great." We came up with a wonderful solution, which was to have a marvelous concert series that took up a fairly large chunk of the student funds. The performers included Otis Redding, Aretha

Franklin, Wilson Pickett, and a bunch of old blues guys performing on campus in free concerts. The Ujamaa Society was happy because I was helping to bring black culture to Wesleyan.

In terms of fulfilling the other duties of my office, I decided to do absolutely nothing and remain as invisible as possible. During the annual Wesleyan scavenger hunt, one of the items on the list was to get my signature, but nobody could do it because they couldn't find me.

Like a lot of people, I had become convinced over the period from midsummer 1966 to the end of autumn 1967 that we were in something like the Age of Aquarius. I wasn't inclined to call it that, but I truly felt like we had leapt through the transom of history into a completely new form of human life. All would now be well.

But then I started seeing increasing evidence that society was simply coming apart. It was suffering from psychedelic toxicity, because what had been a universally shared notion of God-given authority was suddenly something that only the minority believed in. Although there were quite a number of people who could be trusted with having complete self-determination, there were also an awful lot of people who couldn't.

The harm, to the extent that I perceived it for a while, was that a fairly large number of us at Wesleyan were taking LSD in a way that caused the kind of social damage and anxiety that just about everybody was already experiencing without necessarily using LSD on a regular basis. At the time, five hundred micrograms was considered a standard trip, which is far more than I would recommend to neophytes today. I was tripping at least twice a week, generally with others. With regard to the categorical imperative, I knew exactly what it would be like if everybody did what I was doing, because on one level or another, they all were.

And so I was observing behaviors that scared me, and I concluded that something really awful was going to have to happen in order to get people to pay attention to what was now going on in this brave new world we were trying to create as we went along. In fact, that is exactly what happened. Because a year later we got Charles Manson.

In October 1967, I decided that if I did something really outrageous and horrible, it would make the cover of *Newsweek*. More to the point, it would cause everybody to take a hard look at where we were headed in terms of consciousness.

Back on the ranch, I had learned how to make explosives. I think I still have a copy of a remarkable little volume called *The Blaster's Handbook*, a publication that taught you everything you needed to know about making your own high-yield explosives. If you happened to have a dead horse that had frozen solidly to a trail, it instructed you on where to place the charges in order to disperse the carcass.

I mixed up about twenty-five pounds of explosives and put it all into a plastic bag. Then I gathered a bunch of nuts and bolts and ball bearings and shrapnel and started wrapping them all up with duct tape, with the explosives at the core. The whole device wasn't much bigger than about the size of two bowling balls.

My plan was to go sit in the lap of the statue of John Harvard in Harvard Yard and detonate this thing at noon. I didn't tell anyone what I was going to do, but I was acting squirrelly and must have been radiating something weird, because as soon as I got in my car and drove to Cambridge, they began looking for me at Wesleyan.

By then, I had already driven to Cambridge and holed up in a friend's apartment. All the way there, I was as calm as only a crazy person could be. It was like six o'clock in the morning when I arrived. Although I never knew this at the time, my friend must have called the authorities at Wesleyan to tell them what I was about to do. It had been obvious to one and all that I had been up to no good for a while, but I had never said a word to anyone about my plan.

At about eleven o'clock that morning, I got visited by the president of Wesleyan University, the dean of students, the campus psychologist, and one of my closest friends. I didn't show them the explosives, but they already knew about them because I had told my friend about my plans and he had told them when they called.

They immediately snarfed me up and took me back to Connecticut, where they put me into the Institute of Living, a fancy crazy house outside of Hartford. For a couple of weeks, they fed me so much Thorazine that I went to a different part of the phylogenetic chain. I became an invertebrate. I kept begging them to stop, but in order to try to help bring myself back to sanity, I did put together a pretty elaborate model of a whaling ship while I was under the influence.

When I came out, I went right back into the student community. The whole thing was kept hush-hush, because I was kind of an important personage on campus and Wesleyan was trying hard to keep me there as somebody who was not nearly as crazy as I had been. Not many people on campus even knew about any of this. I had just disappeared for a couple of weeks and then I was back and it wasn't much discussed.

For a long time, I didn't want this story to be in the book, because I didn't want to announce to the world that I nearly became America's first suicide bomber. I am pretty sure that I would have done it. At that point, I hadn't even taken any drugs for a while. That was part of the deal. I thought if I quit taking drugs, I would regain my feeling that the world made sense and I wouldn't be so terrified that society was headed over the falls. Because to me, it looked like we were all rowing like crazy in the direction of the precipice. But once I stopped taking drugs, it only got worse. I was like the guy in *The Scream*, the painting by Edvard Munch. I felt just like that character.

It was not suicidal ideation. I didn't want to die. Nor did I want to kill anybody. But I felt like something was going to have to happen to get everybody to stop and take a deep breath so they could see what was going on. What a waste of a life that would have been.

TEN

FAIR-HAIRED BOY

By the end of my senior year at Wesleyan, everybody I knew had just glazed over. We'd had 186 psychological discharges in a student body of 1,100 people. But I still had a special role on campus. The president of the university had plotted out this fairly elaborate political trajectory for himself, and for some reason he thought I was going to be his nexus to the new generation. And so I became his fair-haired boy.

Ted Etherington had been the president of the American Stock Exchange, and now his plan was to go from being president of Wesleyan to the U.S. Senate and then president of the United States. He'd had no idea what he was getting himself into by coming to Wesleyan, which had changed quite a bit since he had gone to school there, and he felt like I was the only person on campus that he could trust. I was weird and I also wasn't, and therefore Ted thought he could communicate with me.

One night in February 1969, he called me up at three o'clock in the morning. I had just taken STP, which by then I had come to enjoy. "John Perry," he said, "you've got to get over to my office immediately.

61

The blacks have taken over Fisk Hall," which was one of the academic buildings. The Ujamaa Society had decided to occupy the building. He said, "We've got to figure out what to do." And I said, "Okay. I could tell you what to do over the phone, but I don't know if that would convince you, so I guess I'll just have to come over."

Meanwhile, I was coming on to the STP, which was a little bit like getting into an elevator that was about to go Mach 3. I went over to Ted's office and said, "Well, here's what I'd do. I'd leave them there. I mean, they're doing it for attention. If it doesn't get them much, they'll quit doing it. It's not like we can't come up with enough spare classroom space. People can always teach classes outdoors if need be."

He took my advice. The sit-in went on for about a day and a half, and then the Ujamaa folks all slunk out of the building. I came down and greeted them as they were leaving the hall and said, "Boy, are you guys lucky. It's a goddamn good thing you were dealing with me and not someone who would have called the cops."

Etherington also had me writing speeches for him in preparation for his planned senatorial bid. Despite all that, he still had to keep me out of sight, sometimes literally.

By then, I was living out in the countryside in a wonderful little house in the woods about three miles from Middletown, and riding my BMW motorcycle to campus. There was a curve in the road that I took every morning and evening and never thought a thing about. One day, I was blazing into that curve running a little late and discovered too late that the previous afternoon they had laid down about two inches of pea-sized gravel. It might as well have been gear lube on the road, because I went right down into it. In and of itself, that would have been bad enough, but it was even worse because I was just wearing cutoff shorts with no shirt, helmet, socks, or shoes.

I was bleeding all over the place, so I got back on the bike and went to the infirmary. I was a horror. There was one area of my back about the size of a dinner plate that had no flesh on it at all. They nursed me back to the point where I asked the doctor what I could wear that wouldn't stick to the wound. He said, "The truth is that you cannot wear anything. You're going to have to leave it open to the air."

Among other things, this meant that I would have to appear in this condition as the sole student representative on the Wesleyan board of directors meeting later that week. And so I did. I walked in there bare-chested, wearing cutoff shorts, looking like a scrofulous beggar from the time of Jesus Christ. To say the least, at that moment Ted Etherington would much rather have had me go right on being invisible.

During the period when I was the dictator of the student body at Wesleyan, a photograph of me smoking a joint appeared on the front page of the *Wesleyan Argus*. That was pretty outrageous, even in those days, but by then I had proven to myself that I could get away with just about anything.

ELEVEN

AN INCREDIBLE WEEK

After graduating with honors in May 1969, I had an incredible week. I had written half of a novel called *The Departures* about a kid who was a lot like me, and his various ancestors and their relationship to the frontier, as well as his gnawing sense that the frontier was over. Paul Horgan took it to Robert Giroux at Farrar, Straus and Giroux, and he bought it for five thousand dollars.

But I didn't necessarily want to buckle down and write the second half of the novel right away. I wanted to be somebody whom people took seriously and was searching for a way to have a legitimate voice. Even though I had been admitted to Harvard Law School—who thankfully had no idea what I had once nearly done on their campus—I'd decided not to go there. I wore a pin that said TURNED DOWN HARVARD.

The other thing that happened during that incredible week had to do with the draft, which I had been thinking about for years. I knew the draft board in Pinedale could not wait to get John Perry Barlow to Saigon, if only to take some of the snot nose out of me. My real fear was that I was going to wind up killing people with whom I did not fundamentally disagree. If the Vietnamese had been attacking us, I might have seen it differently, but we were an occupying army in their country. As the great Muhammad Ali said, "I ain't got no quarrel with them Vietcong," and neither did I.

I'd read enough history to know that Vietnam was not about to become a proxy for China, because the two cultures had hated each other for thousands of years. So it wasn't like the domino theory was going to work. Anyway, I didn't want to do it, and I didn't want to split to Canada.

I thought maybe I would try to become Mexican enough that I could own property there. Mexico wouldn't deport you if you owned property there, but you couldn't own property as a gringo. I would have to become a Mexican citizen. I knew a professor who had a little bed and breakfast in Guanajuato that he was selling for not too much money, and he told me he could take me to the people in charge down there to pay them the *mordida*. I was about to do that when I said to myself, *Wait a minute, Barlow. You can't be a Mexican. You barely speak Spanish.*

So then I thought, *My other choice is two years in a minimum-security federal prison in Safford, Arizona.* Which seemed pretty tolerable. I mean, I could write there. I was sure the company would have been interesting. I had started to accommodate myself to doing that, but then, right as the ultimate hour was rushing toward me, I decided to take one more stab at finding another solution.

I figured I needed several physicians' letters attesting to the fact that I had severe stress-induced asthma. Such a condition does exist, but I did not have it. I went into the offices of three different doctors, stole their letterhead stationery, and created letters using all of the medical terminology I had learned about the subject. Then I went to the Salt Lake City induction center for my physical exam. If I passed they would put me on the bus and I would be in the army.

I showed up in Salt Lake with my letters but also fully prepared to go to prison, because there was no way I was going to let them induct me into the army. I stood in a long circular line where everyone had to get undressed to their skivvies to go through the physical. That was a little weird because I hadn't worn underwear since age fourteen, when I learned that James Bond never wore them, either. So I was naked while everyone was clothed.

At the end of the physical, you saw a doctor whose job it was to review all of the medical petitions. He was an Italian guy from Long Island who didn't really want to be in Salt Lake either, and he read my asthma letters and gave me a 1-Y, which meant I could be drafted only in the event that the Vietnamese actually attacked us. Otherwise, I was free. While remaining perfectly impassive, inside I was actually jumping up and down, head over heels.

As I was walking away, the guy said, "Hey, come back here. I want to take another look at those letters." And I went, "Aw, fuck!" He began looking at them and then started to chuckle.

"You really put a lot of work in on these, didn't you?" And I said, "What makes you say that?" And he said, "If it had been me, I would have used a different typewriter." I had typed all three letters on the same Smith Corona, one with a very distinctive typeface.

Then he said, "This changes things. I'm going to have to ask you to get on the bus." And I said, "I'm not getting on the bus." He said, "What do you mean you're not getting on the bus?" I said, "I'm not getting on the bus. I'm not." And he said, "You mean you're going to resist?" And I said, "Yeah. You're going to have to call the marshals or whatever it is that you do."

He looked at me for a long time. Then he said, "You know, I get about twenty-five cowboys in here every day who cannot wait to go kill gooks in Vietnam. I can't see any good reason to make you kill one." While I would never have gotten away with this at Whitehall Street in New York City, he was clearly no more in favor of the Vietnam War than I was. I had been in a completely decompressed state, but the huge steel band that had been around my entire being for so long suddenly broke.

Another thing that happened during that week was that I got a letter from my friend Kazim Khan, whom I had met at the London School of Economics while I was hanging out there during the summer after my sophomore year. At the LSE, Kazim had been enrolled in a few different courses, but had never gotten his degree, which may have had something to do with the fact that his father was a maharajah near Lucknow, India.

In the letter, Kazim said he was going back home for the first time in twenty years and he would dig it if I came and visited him so he wouldn't feel completely estranged from the world he had been living in. I don't know why he picked me. It was just a simple twist of fate, but he did and so I decided to land on that square.

I had just graduated from college and been admitted to Harvard Law School. I had just sold my novel. I had gotten out of the draft. Pretty much purely on a whim but also because of something that has plagued me throughout my life—coming right to the precipice of success and then backing away from it—I decided to take my book advance and use the money to go to India.

TWELVE

THE JOURNEY EAST

I flew to London and then to Luxembourg and then I got a ticket on what later became the national airlines of the People's Democratic Republic of Yemen, or Southern Yemen, but was then called Brothers Air Services. Their fleet consisted entirely of DC-6Bs, but at least they were pressurized. We made a stopover in Cairo and then lumbered on through the night. I was the only sahib on the plane, and all the Indian passengers put down their seats and spread out these futons and the whole plane suddenly became a living room where people were having tea.

Still, I wasn't even slightly prepared for the culture shock I was about to experience. I got to Bombay, as it was then called, early on a very rainy morning. The monsoons were flowing and I had never seen rain like that. It was raining chains. It was raining ropes. The whole damn country was like a cow pissing on a flat rock, and it was something to behold.

On the bus coming in from the airport, I heared a little commotion in back. The driver stopped and pulled over and went to check it out.

When he came forward again, he was carrying a little stick figure of a man who had just died in the back of the bus. Reverentially, he took him to the side door, put him down gently on the sidewalk, and then drove away. Not much paperwork involved there.

I wasn't quite sure what to do next, so I thought I would go to the best hotel in town and ask them to recommend a place that might be in my budget. I went to the Taj Mahal Palace Hotel, and they sent me to a place that had probably been pretty luxurious back during the days of the Raj but had since fallen on dark and musty times.

I stayed in my room listening to the rain for a couple of days while reading F. Scott Fitzgerald novels. Then I took a train to Lucknow, where I met Kazim's father for the first time. Mohammad Amir Ahmad Khan was a well-known poet and a prominent politician who had been the leader of the All-India Muslim League. He was also a very, very devout Shiite Muslim, and after the Indo-Pakistani War of 1965, the Indian government had decided to freeze all of his assets on religious grounds, and so he could not sell or do anything with all of his treasures.

The family had two palaces. Everybody lived in the city palace in Lucknow, but it had been pretty well stripped of ornamentation by the Hindu government. The one in the countryside was totally extraordinary. It was festooned with things you could have found on the walls of the Victoria and Albert Museum in London. There was Victorian bric-a-brac beyond all comprehension, as well as furnishings and art that dated back to the Moguls.

There was also a fantastic 700,000-volume library of books dating back to the seventh century. Kazim's father could not sell any of them so they were all being eaten by book worms. In that library, I once found the body of a dead bat with a two-and-a-half-foot wingspan.

Kazim's father had many servants in the palace but no money to pay them. Their families had always been in his service, and so they kept the same arrangement they had always had. I had my own suite of rooms and came and went as I pleased. Often I would happen through while Kazim wasn't there, but it was still cool.

I wound up spending a lot of time with Kazim's dad. He was philosophical about how the government had seized all of his property. It made him sad, but he was almost Buddhist in his nonattachment. What counted for him was being the proper servant for the will of Allah. He figured that was what was now happening, just as I did.

I was not on a spiritual pilgrimage in India. Instead, I was doing what I always do, which was hanging out with intent. I went to McLeod Ganj in Dharamsala, where the Dalai Lama had his lamasery in exile. He was there at the time and in the process of giving a cycle of sermons that the Dalai Lama always delivered at a certain age. He spoke in Tibetan so I didn't understand any of it, but it was still interesting just to be there and listen.

The thing that had largely attracted me to Dharamsala was the abandoned Presbyterian mission camp on the top of this mountain where a guy with whom I had shared a dorm suite at Wesleyan was then living. It was a dreadful climb getting up there but from the top of this ridge, I could see the entire Brahmaputra basin, which is vast and beautiful. I trekked up and down and back up to that ridge for about a month and a half.

At one point, I actually found myself on top of a mountain in India with a holy man, a Tibetan lama. He was using one of the cabins to meditate, but was not averse to my coming to talk with him. He knew English pretty well because he had taught for a year at Bryn Mawr, and he was serious about automobile mechanics. In the Tibetan time sense, things happen in synchrony, never with causality except on a spiritual level. Since there is nothing more causal than an automobile engine, the lama felt that if he could understand how it worked, he would have a better insight into how those in the West regarded time.

I didn't trip that much on the mountain because it was superfluous, but I did take acid in Khajuraho, a group of nine-hundred-year-old Hindu and Jain temples south of Jhansi that are famous for their erotic sculptures. In splendid isolation, I tripped in those amazing ruins. Looking at all those bas-reliefs of people screwing in every manner and position imaginable while I was high on acid gave me an entirely new sense of the nature of religion.

I encountered many other hippies on the road; they were pretty common there in those days. Many of them were English and had become highly susceptible to shedding all their Western trappings, putting on dhotis, and wandering across the plains. Sometimes they would be in pretty lousy health, and I would try to persuade them that they needed to come in from the cold for a little while because their bodies had not been adapted by countless generations of parasite gobbling. But they had already cast their lot. They weren't going to have their minds changed by me.

I was in India for nine and a half months, always traveling alone. I did not get laid even once. But I did take out the Dalai Lama's sister a couple of times. She was a schoolteacher, about twenty-five years old. Compared to the Muslims, the Tibetans were pretty easygoing about things like that. I knew this because Kazim had a sister who was about my age, and the family thought it would be a good idea if I took her out to the movies. For some reason, that was something you could do with a girl back then that wouldn't get anyone culturally stirred up. She would go with me, covered up from head to toe in a burka and looking like a giant black tent, and I would sit next to her in the theater with no idea what she was thinking or what she even looked like. Talk about a blind date. There was actually something pretty sexy about it all, but things never went beyond the movies.

As happens sooner or later to almost everyone who travels in India, I eventually got pretty sick. Fortunately, it was toward the end of my time there. By then, I had become transfixed by the burning ghats in Benares on the Ganges where they incinerated the dead bodies. I could not tear myself away from the sight. I don't know if it was then or when I took a fairly lengthy rowboat ride on the Ganges that did it, but I came down with this flu-like thing that had me coughing blood for ages after I got home.

Although my trip to India was not a spiritual pilgrimage like other people back then were doing, very little about my life has not been a form of spiritual exploration. I know that I shed some sort of skin while I was there and came back a different person, in that I could more plainly see the virtues of being more of a Republican than I had been. India, then more than now, was just a grab bag of miscellaneous products of social chaos, some of which were beautiful, some of which were appalling.

A character in E. M. Forster's *A Passage to India* says that India will show you your true self. In that sense, it's like the world's oldest and most complex Rorschach test. Among other things, it showed me that I was much too susceptible to horror and so when I returned to America, I had a different perspective about all that.

In terms of what so many people my age were doing back then by wandering the world in search of spiritual enlightenment, the best insight I can offer is something I was told many years later in Japan by the abbot of the Shunkoin Temple in Kyoto, which is the mother lode of Zen. When I walked in to see him, the abbot was sitting next to a paper wall divider with cranes brushed on it that was thought to be the oldest existing painting in Japan. There were signs everywhere that said NO SMOKING, but the abbot himself was smoking like a furnace. As we were talking, he kept lighting up one cigarette right after another. But then he understood irony.

"You know," he said to me, "we used to see a lot of your kind around here." And I said, "My kind? What would that be?" He said, "You know what I mean. The young Westerner who takes LSD and decides that he is a Buddhist. And doesn't actually have to put in any of the work necessary to become one."

I said, "Guilty as charged. I can't defend myself about that, but did you ever take acid?" And he said, "Yeah, yeah." I said, "So, what were your thoughts on it?" And he said, "I couldn't understand why someone would want to take a brief vacation in a place where I was already living and intended to spend my entire life, if I could make myself capable of it."

COMING HOME

I came back to the United States through Logan International Airport in Boston bearing a life-size Buddha head from Kathmandu that I had filled with a kilo of black Nepalese hashish. I didn't do it for money. I did it in part to determine whether I was going to be a Republican or an outlaw. The lady or the tiger.

The Buddha head was made of bronze, and I had done my best to fashion what appeared to be a bronze bottom for it out of epoxy and stuff I had picked up off the street. I got in the customs line at Logan and soon found myself face-to-face with a big, burly Irish customs guy who was just like a Boston cop. He took one look at me and said, "I'm going to have to look at everything." And I said, "I thought that might be the case."

He started going through all my stuff, and as he did I realized that I had completely forgotten about the piece of typing paper folded up in one of my shirt pockets that had six or eight tabs of Owsley acid inside it. I had brought a bunch with me on the trip, and this was what was left of my supply. I had taken quite a bit of acid in India and had some pretty transcendental experiences. Not the kind you were supposed to have, but they were definitely something.

The customs guy unwrapped the sheet of typewriter paper, found the tabs, and said, "What's this?" And I said, "Well, to be frank, I'm not sure." He said, "The boys in the lab will know." And I was thinking, *There's a test for LSD, really?* Then he gave it to somebody who took it away.

At that point, I was in an incredibly elevated state of mind. I figured that my fate had already been decided: The test for LSD was going to be positive and then they were going to drill into the Buddha head and the next thing I knew, I was going to be in the hoosegow, where I would presumably write the second half of my novel. I had never thought about doing that in India, but I had schlepped the bound first half of the novel around with me. That turned out to be useful because as the search went on, the customs guy knew he had gotten me, and I knew he had gotten me, and so we became extremely collegial. At one point, he found the manuscript and began leafing through it.

"This is pretty good," he said. "I like this."

And I said, "I'm glad you do. I'm supposed to finish it now." The truth was that I was already feeling alarmed about having to finish it because after nine and a half months in India, I was no longer the person who had written the first half.

He kept going through all my things methodically and he found a bunch of infinitesimal ivory elephants that kids in India go blind carving and then put into little seed pods. There are about twenty of them in every pod and if you pour them out, it looks like powder. Then if you look closer, you realize it's actually tiny elephants. He found one of those and said, "Oh, surely this is drugs." And I said, "No, look close. Look close. Closer." And he said, "Holy shit! It's elephants!"

Then the guy from the lab came back from across the hall, and I could hear him laughing the whole way and he said, "Guess what? We blew up the lab with this stuff." I was thinking, *That doesn't sound good.* At that exact moment, the customs guy pulled the Buddha head out of the bottom of my backpack. He looked at it and said, "Funny casting. Do you suppose it's hollow?" And I said, "No." The head itself just radiated dope.

The lab guy suddenly turned slightly more serious and handed the typing paper with the tabs of acid back to me. "I don't know what this is," he said, "but I wouldn't take any of it if I were you." At that moment, the customs guy, still holding the Buddha head, said, "I think we can just let you go."

Now that all my adrenaline had been completely released through my system, I started packing everything back up. The whole time I was shaking like a leaf. As I was getting ready to leave, the customs guy said, "So, if you're writing that novel and you've got some kid carrying dope through customs in it, think of me."

Back in Connecticut, a friend of mine had rented a house in a little beach town called Clinton, the kind of place where orthodontists spent the summer. It was completely dead in the winter and seemed sufficiently out of the fray that I could write the rest of the novel there. At least, that was the concept.

I was getting money from my folks during this period, so I never did sell any of the hash from the Buddha head. I gave a fair amount of it away in the service of getting something done. At one point, someone walked into my living room in Clinton and there were four or five of us there, stoned off our asses. He looked around for a while and then said, "Welcome to the wax museum." Everyone was just that stoned. Petrified.

I worked on the novel but not very successfully. The next spring, in May 1970, I helped bring the Grateful Dead to perform at Wesleyan. The point of the show was to get people out dancing and celebrating and being together because the school was in complete shutdown due to a student strike protesting the war in Vietnam and the bombing of Cambodia. So the Dead played a free show and Sonny Heard, who claimed he was one of their roadies but was just a grotesque parasite who would sometimes carry the band's equipment around, got a gun shoved into his stomach. I loved that, because Sonny Heard was possibly the most vile human being I had ever met.

What happened next was that a set of promoters in New York City decided to duplicate Woodstock at a ski resort in Connecticut called Powder Ridge. It had once been called Powder Hill, but that was too true so they renamed it Powder Ridge. The highest slope had a vertical descent of about four hundred feet, the ski-hill equivalent of a putt-putt course. I used to give night-skiing instruction there to businessmen who wanted to look good over the weekends with their girlfriends.

To play at what was hyped as a huge three-day rock festival on July 31, August 1, and August 2, 1970, the promoters booked Sly and the Family Stone, Delaney and Bonnie, Fleetwood Mac, Melanie, James Taylor, Joe Cocker, the Allman Brothers, Little Richard, Van Morrison, Jethro Tull, Janis Joplin, Chuck Berry, Grand Funk Railroad, Richie Havens, John Sebastian, Spirit, and Ten Years After. After everything had been set up, I volunteered to help out in some capacity, and they put me into a security position. Then a local faction who had looked at Woodstock and decided "Not in our backyard" went to court to stop it. They got some Connecticut judge to issue an injunction declaring that if any of the musicians entered the site, they would immediately be held in contempt of court. Which resulted in none of them showing up.

However, about thirty thousand people came to the festival grounds anyway. Even though there were no acts, they didn't want to leave because they were having a perfectly grand time. Or an imperfectly grand time.

At that point, the professional security company that had been hired decided to leave the premises. In my capacity as the nominal head of the volunteers, I then became head of security, which was like putting the inmates in charge of the institution. I was dealing with problems that didn't come up every day, like a large bunch of kids who had picked a lot of poison ivy, used it to start a bonfire, and then danced around naked in the smoke. They all had to be hospitalized, and I had to find the ambulances to take them there because getting anything onto or off the site was insanely difficult.

For reasons I have never understood, the Connecticut State Police refused to let anyone leave. People were trapped and the entire site quickly became a hippie ghetto. Because I was the head of security at an event that could not be secured, I had to send a lot of the drugs that people had bought on the site to the Connecticut Valley Hospital for chemical analysis so I would know what they had taken. As it turned out, much of it was strychnine and niacin and a bunch of other awful stuff.

The only artist who said "Fuck the judge" and actually performed was Melanie. There was no electricity on the site so I helped rig up some speakers and an amp and a mixing board to the power supply from a Mister Softee ice cream truck, and then she stood on top of it and sang.

The "festival" itself went on for three days, and a lot of people were really messed up. We set aside a big room at the ski resort as a freak-out center, and during the second night, nine hundred people came through. Some of them were stark raving bonkers on shit that has not been available since. We didn't have any doctors or Thorazine to help us bring them back down.

A woman who was standing right next to me, looking at all this, said, "This is so awful, I feel like killing myself." And I said, "I know what you mean. I kind of feel the same way." Except that right after our conversation, she went upstairs and blew her head off. It was yet another time when I was forced to take suicidal ideation seriously. It's statistically high enough to assume that when somebody says something like this, they actually do mean it.

Powder Ridge made Altamont look like a walk in the woods. After three days, the cops finally opened the gates and let people leave. At that point, they were only too happy to do so.

FOURTEEN

NEW YORK, NEW YORK

I spent the summer living in a house that belonged to one of my Wesleyan professors. It was way out in the countryside and looked like a Korean temple, and that was where I finally finished writing the second half of my novel. I submitted it to Farrar, Straus and Giroux and waited. They took their own sweet time to get back to me, so in the fall I moved to New York.

I already knew the city because during my senior year at Wesleyan, I'd shared an apartment on St. Mark's Place in the East Village with a couple of other guys from school, where I went on the weekends. The rent was twenty-eight dollars a month, total. There were so many cockroaches it was like a wildlife preserve.

The apartment was right above the Dom, which Andy Warhol and Paul Morrissey had just turned into a club. I went down there one night to get a drink and who should be singing but Nico. I was ready to follow her anywhere, but not much came of it because she was far too otherworldly for me. I went back to see her the next time she performed there, and that was when I met Rene Ricard.

A poet and a painter who had already appeared in several Warhol films, Rene probably stood about five foot ten and weighed maybe 110 pounds. Back then, not many gay men were as far out of the closet as Rene was. The night I met him, I was wearing leather pants and he came right up to me and said, "Well, hello, cowboy," and I thought, *Well, aren't you a special thing?* And he was. What a piece of work. From that moment on, Rene was desperately in love with me.

At one point during my senior year, I had to go up to Wesleyan because I was the only student member on the committee that decided whether or not students would be expelled, and Rene insisted on coming with me. School was out at the time, so there were only a few people around. I installed Rene in a room with a big bay window on the third floor of my fraternity house.

One of the brothers was a serious climber who was constantly scaling miscellaneous walls around campus. Climbing up the face of the fraternity house that day, he looked through the window and saw Rene lying in bed in a translucent shirt eating strawberries and whipped cream while jerking off. That the climber did not fall off the wall right then still seems like a miracle to me.

Rene was the one who took me to the Factory for the first time. It was a ragged scene. Just about everybody there was shooting speed except for Andy, who never took a drug in his life as far as I could tell. Edie Sedgwick was already gone, but Joe Dallesandro was still there, as was Ultra Violet, who even then had one wing on fire and half her tail shot off but was still astonishing. I was at the Factory quite often on those senior-year weekends, and that was where I began shooting speed.

I'm still surprised that I never came down with hepatitis C. I was also shooting heroin, but I never copped on the street because while I may be crazy, I am not stupid. I always got it from a guy I trusted. You can actually live a long time as a junkie. The problem is that it's really hard to get a truly reliable standardized titration. I went through heroin withdrawal and it was not fun, but then as Mountain Girl once said to me, "You're the best little quitter I know."

I didn't think shooting crank was glamorous. When everybody at the Factory started shooting up horse as well, I looked around one day and it seemed like all these brilliant, sparkly people had gone gray and lusterless. I just thought, *Fuck, I don't want to be one of them.* There wasn't anything glamorous about shooting heroin, either. It was just a way to pass the time. In a situation like that, you're not just killing time, you're murdering it.

The Factory itself was in fact exactly that—a factory. The name wasn't a metaphor, because they were manufacturing art. Andy would have these ideas and then say what he wanted done, and we'd all busily set about doing it. There are a couple of Warhol screen prints on permanent display at the Museum of Modern Art that I worked on.

Having a conversation with Andy back then wasn't exactly like having a normal conversation, because the actual syllables leaving his lips were few and far between. However, he did have these very subtle emotive qualities that made it easier to understand him. I didn't think of him as a master manipulator of people except in the sense that the sun is a master manipulator of planets. Andy was the white dwarf neutron star at the core of the entire scene. All the people around him were wildly flamboyant characters who talked all the goddamn time. But not Andy. He was just *there,* and he attracted all these other colorful orbital bodies. I was happy to be one of them for a spell. I wasn't particularly attracted to the Factory because it was an art scene. I was attracted to it because it was one hell of a scene.

When I moved back to New York again, in the fall of 1970, I had an especially sweet deal. I was staying with this gay couple, an older man and a younger man, who lived in a duplex at the Hotel des Artistes at 1 West Sixty-Seventh Street, near Central Park. They also had a farm in Putney, Vermont, where they would go all the time, and they told me I could be their house sitter in the city. The older man had been a colleague of my girlfriend's father during the war so they were almost like family.

The couple would periodically throw these parties where big-deal guys who happened to be closeted gays would come down from their family mansions in Greenwich, Connecticut, so they could let their hair down. Believe it or not, I was kind of cute back then, and the couple paid me to mince around at these gatherings, giving the impression that they were both fucking me so I wasn't quite available to anyone else. I was just supposed to flirt with the guests and make them happy that way. By doing this, I think I learned something about what it was like to be a woman. These men would come on to me, and I would respond by flirting with them in a girlish sort of way. So for me, it was actually a wonderful experience.

The parties themselves were incredible. Gay life in pre-Stonewall America was a horrible thing. It really was. These were all good guys who really did love their families, but the only time they could ever be themselves was when they came to these parties in the city.

The other thing that was going on while I was living at the Hotel des Artistes was that oral birth control pills were pretty much universally available for the first time. Radical feminists had told women that they were no different from men and therefore should be just as sexually ravenous. Aside from syphilis, there were no major sexually transmitted diseases. There were also lots of quaaludes, which had a somewhat limited utility because, as someone once said, they turned women into animals and men into vegetables. Happy vegetables, but still.

All in all, it was a hell of a good time to be in New York, which for me has always been the capital of magic and longing. Back then, New York was a great place to get laid, but not a great place to stay laid, and so I was seeing a pretty fair amount of action.

Then I went to this party where I met some Argentinian rich boys from good families who told me they were bringing kilos of pure pharmaceutical-grade cocaine into the United States. One of them said they were having a difficult time finding a distribution network. I thought about their problem and asked a friend of mine who lived in Spanish Harlem if she knew anybody who dealt cocaine, and she said she did.

Because my Spanish was really shitty and barely *turista,* I took her as my interpreter and met with a couple of Puerto Rican guys who were no joke, man. I said, "I will bring you a kilo of cocaine that I have divided into honest ounces and have not cut or touched in any way. This is an affordable amount for you guys, right?" They said it was, and then I told them they could buy as many ounces as they could afford. What they then did with the stuff was not my business. What I did was provide them with pure coke.

The first time we did a deal, they bought the whole kilo for about six or eight grand in cash, mostly in hundreds. Before the money changed hands, they did some themselves to see if it was really good. Generally, I was not doing any of it. I was just into the danger.

I brought the money to the Argentinian guys and took my cut, which was 20 percent. The money wasn't all that important to me, and I thought 20 percent was a pretty modest fee, considering I had actually put much more work into it than they had.

This began happening on a weekly basis. My theory was that once the Puerto Rican guys established that I really was doing what I said, I would be too valuable for them to waste. I knew that every time I rode away from them on my BMW with a bunch of their cash in my pocket as they were holding the cocaine, the temptation to blang me off my motorcycle had to be there. By then, I had begun carrying a gun with me in certain parts of the city. It was a .38 FBI model and because this was New York City, I was supposed to have it registered but I did not. The Puerto Rican guys were packing heat as well. They knew I was armed because I was behaving in a way that would indicate I was either truly crazy or I was armed.

This all went on for the better part of three months, until a motorcycle magazine asked me to write an article about taking a brand-new BMW motorcycle across the country and then back again. The whole time, I had been waiting for Farrar, Straus and Giroux to figure out what they were going to do with my novel. But as I geared up to leave, I still hadn't heard anything from them.

While I was on that cross-country trip, I had more than one *Easy Rider* moment. In New Jersey, a no-necked barbarian tried to kill me by running my bike off the road with his Dodge Super Bee muscle car. When I scrambled off into the bush where he couldn't follow, he came out of his car with a pistol. He pointed it at me, and then his wife, who had apparently been asleep in the back seat, rose up and started shouting at him. He shook his head, threw the gun down in the front seat, got back into the car, and drove away. We never even said a single word to each other.

I kept riding west until I got to Rawlins, Wyoming, a truly godforsaken town in the middle of the state. It's a dreadful place, best known as the home of the Wyoming State Penitentiary. The only good thing about Rawlins was a now long-gone place called the Flame Café, which was where my parents had liked to stop while driving down to Cheyenne.

I had a warm, familial feeling about the Flame Café because it was an old haunt for me. But this time when I walked through the front door, I was no longer the fair-haired boy who used to come in with Senator Barlow. I had long hair, I was in my motorcycle leathers, and I had been riding in the rain for an hour or so. I was a freak. I was the other. I was somebody who was against the war in Vietnam. I was the reason that America was no longer great.

I sat down at a table and ordered the lamb roast, and it took a really long time coming. There also seemed to be a fair amount of commotion going on in the kitchen along with a lot of dark laughter. Eventually, the waitress came out with this skinned raw lamb's head with the eyes still in it, lying in a pool of blood, on a stainless steel platter. She put it down in front of me.

Everyone in the restaurant was watching me. I knew I was in a situation where everyone could have just fucking beaten me to death and nobody would have ever found out. What they wanted me to do was react and start shouting. Instead, I just got to my feet and walked very slowly and carefully through the door. Then I got back on my bike and rode like hell out of Rawlins, Wyoming.

I made it to California and then rode back to the East Coast, only to learn that Farrar, Straus and Giroux had given me back my novel. I found an agent who began shopping it around again, but it just kept getting rejected. The only consolation was that the motorcycle magazine liked my article so much that they let me keep the bike.

What came next for me was a period of utter confusion and massive self-doubt. I moved in with an ex-girlfriend with whom I had once been obsessed. Although we were no longer in a state of connubial bliss, we were sharing a bed in a nondescript apartment in a nondescript building in Middletown.

I began thinking that maybe I could reapply to Harvard Law School, but my desire to do that had been considerably reduced by the realization that if I became a lawyer, my job would be to constantly sow doubt, fear, paranoia, and distrust. I knew I wouldn't be any good at doing that because it was something I wouldn't have wanted to be good at. I was really at loose ends with no idea what I was now supposed to do with my life.

FIFTEEN

MEXICALI BLUES

I drove out to California in late December and stayed there through January, and that was when I really got to know Jon McIntire. By then, Robert Hunter and Jerry Garcia had already written "Uncle John's Band" about him, and he was about to become the manager of the Grateful Dead.

Physically, he was a classically beautiful man in the post-Raphaelite style. He had long flowing blond hair, aristocratic features, and the bearing of one of King Arthur's Knights of the Round Table. It was bumpkin nobility, the kind that only comes from truly being from the provinces. I always felt like a complete barbarian around him because Jon was such a ridiculously elegant person in the way he carried himself.

Jon was from Belleville, Illinois. He had gone to Washington University in St. Louis and so was well educated and extremely literate but also an astonishingly adept autodidact. He then went to San Francisco State, where he met Rock Scully and studied German phenomenology. That was where he also met Rock's friend Danny Rifkin, who introduced Jon to the Dead.

Part of what brought us together was that I was studying German phenomenology myself and had just been reading Edmund Husserl and Martin Heidegger and that whole sick crew. It kind of blew Jon away that there was anyone else who actually knew anything about any of this, especially someone wearing a cowboy hat.

Within the Grateful Dead scene itself, very few people knew Jon was gay. Garcia must have known, but he couldn't have cared less. The real dominant strain in the culture of the band, which few people recognize, came straight out of Pendleton, Oregon, through roadies like Rex Jackson and the Hagen brothers, who were real cowboys and as macho as they came.

Jon himself was not a lookist. It was always the other party's mind that interested him. For him, it was always about love rather than cruising. Jon also never wanted to have a relationship with anybody but a straight guy that he had somehow managed to turn.

I went to see the Dead on New Year's Eve at Winterland and was living at Weir's until Jon lured me over to his place. I was staying there with him when he and Weir and I cooked up a plot to go to Mexico together in a three-cylinder, two-stroke Saab that broke down during our trip every day at the exact same time, about four-thirty or five in the afternoon.

I would be standing by the side of the road with the hood up alongside all these solemn Mexicans in straw hats and white shirts who had just seemed to suddenly precipitate out of thin air so they could look at this engine that was not at all familiar to them. At one point, I had to sew the fan belt together so we could keep on driving. We stayed in pretty cheap hotels and were *muy borracho* a good deal of the time, because we were on an expedition. We were not smoking too much weed, but we were snorting a little blow.

One night, we were all trying to get into a very fancy nightclub in Mexico City. We told them we were Los Grateful Dios, but they didn't know anything about that. Then we told them that we were Los Rolling Stones. They knew about them but were not particularly impressed. So then we told them we were with Los Creedence Clearwater Revival and they went nuts. They loved them. Everywhere we went in Mexico, we heard Creedence.

I was sitting in the Saab in a *mercado* in Guadalajara one day when I heard Kris Kristofferson singing "Sunday Morning Coming Down" on the radio. The song totally blew me away because I could relate to the story of it so completely. I had never written any lyrics before, but that song inspired me to think that maybe I could.

Weir had a gig back in the United States and so we reluctantly sent him off. Jon really wanted something to happen with me, and I was thinking, "Better to be bisexual, surely." I figured this would more than double my opportunities because I could always get laid with a guy.

We eventually ended up in this completely isolated village called Puerto Angel on the Gulf of Tehuantepec, about 150 hard miles of dirt from Oaxaca. The only electricity in the town was devoted to running the beer coolers and the jukebox at the cantina, which blared out wall-to-wall Los Creedence at maximum volume.

I decided this was the time for me to find out about this whole bisexuality thing. Jon and I gave it a shot, but it was absolutely not working for me. We got into bed together and did a lot of naked thrashing about but not much more because it all felt too weird. Jon had stubble on his face and it didn't smell right because he was a guy. We kissed each other because we could do that, but I didn't get the feeling that it was ever going to be anything but strange.

Jon was a dramatic fellow and after it didn't happen between us, he pouted for a while. Then we got drunk together and had a conversation about it and the cloud lifted and we became even deeper friends than we had been before.

We returned to San Francisco, and I drove back to Wyoming in my El Camino. I stayed with my folks for a little while and then flew back to Connecticut, where I was still living in that nondescript apartment with the girlfriend with whom I was not having sex. And that was where I eventually sat down and wrote the lyrics to "Mexicali Blues."

SIXTEEN

SUGAR MAGNOLIA

In February 1971, the promoter Howard Stein brought the Grateful Dead to the Capitol Theatre in Port Chester, New York, to perform a series of shows. He decided to invite the entire Dead family to come along and rented a great big old mansion in Dutchess County, where we all stayed like kids in a dormitory. I was in a room with Billy Kreutzmann and Ramrod, and Kreutzmann told me he was going to kill me if I didn't stop fucking this smoking-hot girl who was so beautiful that it really felt sublime to have sex with her even though we were in the same room as Kreutzmann and Ramrod.

It was a ten-day stand in Port Chester, and at one point in the proceedings, Rex Jackson turned me upside down and shook me by my heels because he thought I might have some cocaine on me that he very much wanted to snort at that moment. As it happened, I did not.

One night during the run, Robert Hunter and Weir were trying to work on a song in a back room at the Capitol Theatre, and it was not going well at all. This came as no surprise to me because Hunter is irascible and Bobby is impossible. Bobby is lovely and sweet and smart and wonderful and talented and so well qualified to be my official best friend, but he can sometimes be a pain in the ass. He is also pretty much not controllable in any way. You can't tell Weir to do anything. If you do, you have just decreased your chances that he will do it.

I had already been rendered speechless by Hunter's incredible song-writing ability, as well as his special relationship with Garcia. The song that Hunter and Bobby were working on in the back room that night was "Sugar Magnolia," which was about Bobby's girlfriend Frankie. Weir kept changing the words because he thought he had better ones, and Hunter did not believe in making deals on shit like that.

All of a sudden, Hunter whirled on me and said, "Why don't you write with him? At least you like him." And I said, "I don't know that I know how to write songs." He said, "I've read your poetry. That's pretty good. I think you'd be able do this." And I said, "I suspect songwriting is really different." And he said, "Oh, it is, but you'll probably figure it out. In any case, I'm not writing with him anymore."

Weir looked at me and said, "What do you think?" And I said, "I'd certainly be willing to give it a try." At the time, I was still thinking about how listening to "Sunday Morning Coming Down" had affected me when I had been in Mexico.

After the shows were over, I returned to that nondescript apartment in Middletown and got myself a bottle of Wild Turkey. I drank up most of it and wrote "Mexicali Blues" in a day and sent it to Weir, who was by no means certain that he liked it.

These days, I know it would be tricky to write a song referring to a presumably physical relationship with a girl who was just fourteen years old. Even though everything in the song was purely imaginary, I did it because Weir had specifically asked me to write a cowboy song. Hoping that maybe something would be there, I just turned on the song faucet. I still like the last verse:

Is there anything a man don't stand to lose
When he lets a woman hold him in her hands?

He just might find himself out there on horseback in the dark
Just ridin' and runnin' across those desert sands

I had not sung Weir the melody, and that was the last time that ever happened because he wrote a very different one for it. The original was a lot more like "Sunday Morning Coming Down" and kind of bleak. Weir made it more rhythmic and rapid, which was really pretty surprising to me. I ended up watching him do this in a studio in San Francisco.

Before any of this happened, I had been sleeping with a woman who was the head of public relations at Warner Bros. Records and musing about how I was going to make enough money to survive. I was talking to her about needing some sort of job, and she said, "You know, we could stand having somebody who is wired into the scene in San Francisco, if you wanted to do that with the Dead for us." So I said, "Okay. That sounds good." I would have been an underassistant West Coast promotion man, and what's not to like about that? All I would have had to do was hang out with the band.

I was on my way to take the job when I got waylaid at the ranch. My father had suffered a stroke several years before and was in rough shape. He was in a wheelchair most of the time, and my mother was trying to run the ranch without ever leaving the office and the foreman was trying to run it without ever going in there. They had a bunch of debt, because my father was no longer the businessman he had once been and instead had become something of a philistine. He liked flashy bling stuff and going to Las Vegas, and he threw money around because he wanted to be worth a lot more than he could ever make from running a cattle ranch. He also gambled and lost a lot of money on the commodity exchanges. Had my father not done that, he would have been in the black. But by the time I got there in March 1971, we were more than half a million dollars in the red, which was a lot of money back then. It was a mess.

When I arrived on the ranch, seven people were living and working there full-time. Slowly, I began to realize that I had to stay there. I wanted to put the Bar Cross in order so I could sell it and bail out my parents. I figured it for a short-term affair, but then I got terribly into it.

I was doing a real estate tour of the ranch one day with a bunch of prospective buyers and agents. At the end of it, one of the Realtors took me aside and said, "John Perry, I think you've got to ask yourself if you really want to sell this place, because you just told these people everything that's wrong with it." Categorically, I had just made the worst sales pitch he had ever heard. And I thought, *You know, he's right.*

A lot of whether I could turn the ranch around would depend on John Hay, who had been my father's banker and so was now my banker as well. He was a wise old Scotsman, and I needed him to loan me money. I went down to see him and said, "I've decided that I want to go on ranching on the Bar Cross for as long as I can." And he said, "If you want my opinion, John Perry, it won't be very long. I mean, I give you a year and a half, two years at the most. Less if your father dies, which I think he will."

Then he said, "I've got examiners I have to stay ahead of, but I can probably develop enough of a smoke screen so you can do this if you want to for as long as you can and I can." So we proceeded from there. It was really, really tough, because I was packing all that debt. I was also selling on one of the last free markets that was actually somewhat fixed in favor of the buyers. The only thing I had any control over were the expenses.

At the Bar Cross, our business model was to put cows up on the forest reserve with the bulls, so they would become pregnant over the course of the summer. Then they'd come back down, and any of them that were not pregnant got shipped to be slaughtered. The mother cows varied from three to fifteen years old. The ones that kept giving birth lived. They were in a competition without ever knowing what the rules were.

During the calving season, we'd have about eleven hundred mother cows on the ranch giving birth at the same time. In addition to that, another two hundred or so replacement heifers were being brought in as well. It was a pretty big ranch, and the cattle were scattered in various large fields where I was feeding them.

Winter on the Bar Cross would begin in October, but it could snow as early as July because the elevation is so high. I saw it happen. All these calves were born in February and March, which was awful because it would be freezing cold and I'd be bumping around on feed trail tracks in the middle of the night trying to make sure that all the calves were coming out all right.

The heifers that had never calved before were pretty sensitive about getting the first one out, so I had to get up at two or three o'clock in the morning to check on them. If the birth was not going well, I would run them into the calving barn and go find my foreman, and then we'd put them in a stanchion and pull the calf out ourselves, unless the heifer needed a Cesarean, in which case I would call the vet. But I even had to do several of those myself and somehow managed to deliver the calves successfully.

We'd always start vaccinating and branding in the spring. Our biggest branding event was held in May, when, over the course of three days, we would brand about six or seven hundred calves. Then we'd have another one-day session in June, where we'd brand another couple hundred, and a third session in July, where we'd brand sixty to a hundred.

On branding day, we'd usually get up at about four-thirty or five so we could take the cows out of the meadows at sunup. By about seven-thirty, we'd be running them through the chute. Vaccinations would take a good part of the morning, but we would try to brand several hundred before lunch and then another couple hundred in the afternoon.

Just about everybody in the Cora Valley would come to help us brand in May. We would usually do it on Mother's Day weekend, which gave it a kind of perverse quality that I really liked. This was when we would move all our cows out of the meadows and onto their pastures out in the sagebrush. We always did the big May branding down at the Finn place, because it was centrally located to all of the meadows and various pastures and had a good chute system. We'd usually eat lunch down there as well, rather than going all the way back to the main house.

I don't think I have ever gone to a completely sober branding. There was a lot of variation between one ranch and another as to just how un-sober it got. At some ranches everyone would start out drunk, but that was never the way we did it. Still, I can remember years on the Bar Cross when, by the end of the day, every single person there was drunk.

Just how drunk people got while they were branding always depended on whether or not hard liquor was being consumed. There was almost always a lot of beer around, but sometimes there would also be several bottles of whiskey sitting on the front seat of a pickup truck, and that would give the undertaking a whole different flavor. I still associate alcohol with branding because, back then, alcohol and gasoline were pretty much the two substances that Sublette County ran on.

While we were branding, a lot of other things would be going on as well. Some young guy on the crew would take a liking to a girl who had just come to cook in the main house. They'd want to wrestle calves together, and I'd have to split them up. Somebody would pass out in the front seat of his pickup or fall off his horse and break his arm. A great big hailstorm would hit right in the middle of everything, or someone would get themselves in a major wreck on the highway. So it was never exactly dull.

While I was living on the ranch, I always kept a diary. Here's a typical entry for a branding day:

We emerged mounted at five-twenty A.M. The morning was cool, even cold and damp. The main event of the rodeo occurred as we were trying to corral the Finn bunch. Because of the narrow gate and other factors unknown to us but worrisome to the bovine mind, this is always a tough job. But never have we had the entire bunch come back at us like they did this morning. They scattered like dandelion fluff in a gale and weren't contained until eight A.M. After that, however, things improved. With five sets of wrestlers, we went through them like shit through a frog and were done by eleven-thirty. The count was two hundred and seven cows and two hundred and five calves, of which a hundred and two were steers. A hundred and forty-three were crossbreds. The beer consumed during the hour before lunch made us all too listless to be useful after it was over. I then went down and fixed a loose bolt on a friend's tractor in the afternoon.

Around the end of October, I'd ship all the calves to whomever I'd sold them to, and they would be finished out on grass on another ranch because that was what the market had started to demand. It became a lot cheaper to grass-feed beef than it was to grain-feed them. I would get paid when I delivered the calves to whomever would raise them to full-grown yearlings and then they would turn them over to somebody else who also would keep them for another six months and finish them out. I was at the mercy of the free market in terms of fuel, of which the Bar Cross burned a lot.

But it felt right for me to be living there again. The land itself was hilly, and about 15,000 acres of it was government land to which we had exclusive grazing rights. The Bar Cross itself was 7,500 acres of fairly steep hills that were bare but for sagebrush and a large open alluvial plain through which the New Fork River runs.

Our deeded property included the head of the creek, and there was a dam on New Fork Lake, which my grandfather had built, that irrigated a much larger area. There were 17,000 acre-feet of water on top of that lake, and I sat on the commission that adjudicated those water rights. It was one of the most interesting things I ever did because it turns out people will kill one another over water. They really will. So we had to be judicious in how we allocated it all.

A lot of folks there had looked at me as an outsider back when I had first left to go off to Fountain Valley, and their feelings had not changed in the ensuing period of time. Once I was back living on the Bar Cross, I made matters somewhat worse by publicly going out with a seventeen-year-old girl from Pinedale High School. She was a wonderful person and her father liked me, but everyone else in town just thought of it as further evidence that John Perry Barlow was not like them. Which I most certainly was not.

SEVENTEEN

LOOKS LIKE RAIN

In January 1972, Weir came out to the Bar Cross so we could write songs together for his first solo album. That was when he saw the ghost.

Actually, it was his dog who first discovered the ghost. Bobby had brought with him a young malamute named Moondog who wasn't even a year old. They were both staying with me in an old homestead ranch house at the Finn place, across the ditch from the cabin where I had gone to school. Suddenly, at about three in the morning, the dog did a couple of revolutions around the kitchen and left a dog-high line of liquid shit around the full circumference of the room. The dog had been completely freaked out by something so we got up and dealt with that, got the dog situated outside, and went back to sleep.

The ghost itself had deviled me ever since I had moved into the Finn place. It was the practice of this ghost to manifest itself invisibly but palpably at the end of my bed and look at me in a stark way. It seemed like a man, and I had experienced it many times while sleeping.

After the first few times, I had come to the conclusion that the damn thing wasn't going to do anything but stand there and look at me.

On this night, though, Weir encountered the ghost at the end of his bed. He woke up in horror and as soon as he was out of its thrall, he called up Rolling Thunder, a shaman to the Eastern Shoshone, who was living in a trailer house on an Indian reservation near Carlin, Nevada. By then, Rolling Thunder had decided that he liked being the darling of rock stars, and so he was more than happy to talk to Bobby, even at such an ungodly hour of the night.

Weir said, "I've just experienced a ghost and it scares me. What should I do?" Rolling Thunder said, "You can exorcise this ghost. I would bet that if it's a ranch you are on, there are cedar fence posts somewhere nearby because they last a lot longer than regular fence posts." Rolling Thunder told Weir that he should get a drawknife and peel the fence posts and then take all the bark peelings and put them in a coffee can. After he had punched holes in the side of the can and set the bark peelings on fire, he should go around the house with it and begin singing a Shoshone chant that Rolling Thunder started teaching him.

Now, it was true that there were cedar fence posts nearby, but they were all under about three feet of snow. So Bobby said, "No, no, no. Is there something I can do with less work?" And Rolling Thunder said, "You could take a box of stick matches and get a plate and burn the entire box and then grind them up until they are a fine carbon powder and then smear it all over your face." And Weir said, "That sounds doable."

So he went and got a box of stick matches from the kitchen and did just that. I only found out about what he had done when I went into his bedroom at six-thirty in the morning to wake him up so we could go feed the cattle together. Weir came up out of bed looking like Al Jolson about to break into "My Mammy."

It was one of those rare moments in my life when I was totally speechless. I had seen him earlier in the night when he was dealing with the dog, and he sure as shit hadn't looked like that.

We were feeding about eight hundred cows every morning and then writing songs in the afternoon and evening. We were still trying to figure out how to do this together. Bobby would sit there with a guitar and I would sit there with a legal pad.

We began with "Black-Throated Wind." Oddly enough, I had written the chorus while riding on a bus to the airport in Kathmandu and not anywhere near drowning in the Mother American night. If anything, I was drowning in the weird Nepali night. It was the first thing that ever showed up that seemed like it might be part of a song and not a poem.

I sang those lines for Weir, and he perversely put them into a different melodic setting than I'd just sung. I then wrote the rest of the lyrics. The last few verses were like a dental extraction. They have grown on me over the years, but at the time, it was all perspiration and no inspiration and wretchedly painful. I do think the line "You ain't gonna learn what you don't want to know" is actually pretty good.

Weir and I were drinking Wild Turkey one night, which we did all the time because I don't think Bobby and I ever wrote a song together when we were not drinking Wild Turkey, and up on the wall of the cabin, I had this old-timey N. C. Wyeth print of an Indian with his hands out. Weir looked at the print and said, "You know what he's saying, right?" I said, "No, what?" And he said, "Looks like rain."

I thought that was hilarious. Only Weir would say that. It was a total Weir-ism. And it led to "Looks Like Rain." He planted the seed, even though at that point my experience with "being in love" was pretty much restricted to Shakespeare, opera, and novels by women with three names from the southern states in which someone would swoon. I had often thought about what actually being in that sort of love would be like and had concluded that it was a fiction humans had created to make us all feel more painfully aware of our limitations.

In a sense, the lyrics were fraudulent because I was not writing from experience. But I was writing from a kind of foreknowledge, and it all came to me relatively easily. I then did something that I had sworn after "Mexicali Blues" I would never do again, which was just give the lyrics to Bobby without any sense of where they ought to go or what the song should sound like. But Bobby did an incredibly beautiful job of writing the melody, and I was delighted when I heard it.

Many years later, the Dead were playing "Looks Like Rain" in Nassau Coliseum, and I was snuggled up against a woman with whom I actually was in that kind of love. I suddenly realized who this song had been composed for and who it was that I felt this way about. I started singing it to her and said, "I swear I wrote this for you many years ago."

EIGHTEEN

CASSIDY

Cassidy Law was one month old when I first met her in 1970 on a flea-bitten little ranch called the Rucka Rucka that Weir had out in the headwaters of the Nicasio Valley in west Marin County. He was living out there with Cassidy's mother, Eileen, the patron saint of the Deadheads, his girlfriend Frankie, Rex Jackson (after whom the Rex Foundation was named), and Sonny Heard, also known as the world's most hated person.

The Rucka Rucka was thirty-seven acres of pure dust. There was a ranch right across the highway where all the horses came down with hydrophobia. I mean, can you think of anything scarier than a rabid horse? Weir had an absolutely useless hammerhead Appaloosa stud and a psychotic peacock that would attack you whenever you came out the front door. Bobby kept a two-by-four right next to it so you could fend off the peacock. But he advised you not to kill it. Just hit it.

By the time I got to the Rucka Rucka after my *Easy Rider* motorcycle journey across America, I was in the right raw mood for the place. I remember Eileen holding her beautiful baby girl and hearing the chords Bobby had strung together on the night that Cassidy had been born. Crouched on the bare boards of the kitchen floor in the late afternoon sun, he whanged them out for me, and they rang like the bells of hell in my head for the next two years.

At the Rucka Rucka, Bobby and I put together the melody scheme of "Cassidy," but I wrote the lyrics in February 1972 while bulldozing snowdrifts out of stockyards on the ranch in a cloud of whirling ice crystals. Hypnotized by the steady howl of the bulldozer's engine and the repeating chords of "Cassidy," I thought a lot about my father and what we were and had been to each other.

For some reason, I also started thinking about Neal Cassady, who was then four years dead but still charging around America on the hot wheels of legend. Somewhere in there the words to the song arrived, complete and intact, and I found myself singing the song as though I'd known it for years.

My father was then in a hospital in Salt Lake City. It looked like he was going to die, so I knew I had to be there with him. My good friend Alan Trist, who ran Ice Nine Publishing for the Dead for years, had been staying with me on the ranch, and he decided to come along with me. It was snowing like crazy, but we were in my Chevy Blazer and I knew I could always put it into four-wheel drive if I had to.

When we got to La Barge, Wyoming, a godforsaken town about sixty miles south of Pinedale, we learned the road had been closed because of all the snowdrifts. I decided we just had to bomb our way through. It got extremely hairy. There were no other cars on the highway and I couldn't see the lane markers, but I could see the reflector posts. And so I drove in these conditions all the way from La Barge to Interstate 80. Alan is very English in the best sense of the term. At one point, he said, in his classic fashion, "You know, it occurs to me, Barlow, that we could die out here."

When I finally managed to get to my father's bedside in the hospital in Salt Lake City, he was actually doing pretty well. The thing about my dad was that he had seven brothers and all but two of them died of the same genetic degenerative cardio ailment. What happens eventually with this condition is that the person suffering from it goes into ventricular fibrillation. One of his brothers had dropped dead that way at seventeen. There was one living brother who hadn't made it there to see him yet, and I felt like that was the reason my father didn't die that night. By then, he had already made his peace with it and was well prepared to do so.

I stayed there with him, and the next night at about four-thirty in the morning, his heart monitor went steady and my father died. I would have let him go, but because I knew he wanted to see his brother, I ran to get the nurses and they got the doctor to hit him with the paddles.

It takes a while for someone to return from death. Longer than two minutes, shorter than three days. So there was a period when I was looking deeply into my father's face for what seemed like a long time waiting for him to come back. And then he opened his eyes and looked up at me with a radiant smile and said, "Why, John Perry, are *you* still alive?"

I could tell that my father had been somewhere because he had a completely different light in his eyes. The next day, his heart self-regularized and went back to beating normally. And so I was inclined to think some kind of miracle had taken place that would allow me to go out to California so I could work with Bobby.

I did this and then spent the next five days or so writing the balance of Bobby's solo album *Ace*. Jerry Garcia and Phil Lesh were working with David Crosby on his solo album in the same studio, and so *Ace* is essentially the Grateful Dead studio album of that period, because both Jerry and Phil as well as Bill Kreutzmann are on many of the tracks.

My father finally passed and so I had to head back to Salt Lake, but Bobby still needed one more song for the album. I stayed up all night with Frankie Weir, who fed me Wild Turkey and cocaine and made me write the fairly dreadful "Walk in the Sunshine." I also wrote a song based on Pär Lagerkvist's *The Dwarf* called "The Dwarf" that included the lyrics "I'm not a tall man / I'm a small man." It was about a horrible little Renaissance court dwarf who had no one's interests at heart. I gave it to Bobby, and so he was greatly relieved when I showed him the only slightly less terrible "Walk in the Sunshine," and I was free to go.

My father was sixty-eight years old when he died on February 24, 1972. We buried him in Pinedale on February 29, 1972, a leap day. The funeral itself was a little tricky because the cemetery was covered by four feet of snow. There was a service in the high school auditorium that about 1,200 people attended in a town where only 1,200 lived. My father was widely mourned. People came from all over Wyoming and beyond.

I didn't speak at his service, which seems funny to me now. I think I was in a daze. To a large extent, I was just letting it all happen around me. A lot of people seemed to have a passionate interest in having the service done in a certain way, and I was okay with whatever they wanted. But for some reason I didn't want to get too involved myself.

I took it all pretty hard, because after the stroke had taken out the rational part of my father's brain, there was all this stuff going on in the irrational part that was really lovely. I felt I'd had what now seemed an all-too-short time of actually knowing who he was and being able to talk to him about things that were not absolutely material and literal. What he had always wanted to talk to me about before the stroke was money, business, cattle, and water. But once the filter was gone, he was willing to talk to me about what it really meant to be alive.

He apologized for having made fun of me when I told him that I was still trying to find myself, because he had now finally found himself. And he told me that he loved me, which he had never said before, and I told him that I loved him. That this did not make either of us uncomfortable was truly amazing to me.

NINETEEN

JOHN F. KENNEDY, JR.

In the summer of 1977, John F. Kennedy, Jr., was about to turn seventeen years old. He was out of Secret Service protection and didn't have constant babysitting anymore. He was like a gigantic golden Lab puppy and needed a lot of running room, which was not something he could find at home on 1040 Fifth Avenue. As a consequence, he was being a pest and doing shit like mixing up five gallons of wallpaper paste and then pouring it down the mail chute.

His mother was anxious because there was no man around to control him. Her real fear was that John was going to get himself into serious trouble because he was always pushing the envelope. She decided that he needed to be placed in a slightly secret location far from public view and came up with the very Democratic idea of putting him with the Youth Conservation Corps in Yellowstone National Park. But that did not work out well. The other kids were all from the inner city but not from the part of the inner city that he was from. It just wasn't happening for him, and the press had picked up on the fact that he was there.

But his mother still did not want to bring him in from the cold. Both of his families, the Bouviers and the Kennedys, had a practice of tossing their sons out at a certain point without much ceremony. She decided it might be a good idea to put him on a ranch somewhere. So she called up Representative Teno Roncalio, who was dear to her heart because while serving as the chairman of the Wyoming delegation, he had essentially handed the nomination for president to John F. Kennedy by delivering the state to him at the 1960 Democratic National Convention.

Teno, who had helped raise me, was a badda-bing Rat Pack guy. He was a ladies' man to the max and drove the first Corvette Stingray I ever saw. My father basically apprenticed me to him when I was twelve or thirteen years old, because I wanted to ski all the time and my dad didn't want to learn how. Teno was always going off skiing and liked me, and so he became like an uncle to me.

John's mother called Teno and said, "Do you have a friend who has a ranch that John could work on?" And Teno said, "I've got just your guy." As it happened, at the time she had that conversation with Teno, her daughter, Caroline, was going out with my good friend Tom Carney, whose family owned a ranch up the Green River from the Bar Cross.

Tom was having dinner at Jackie's apartment that same night and she said, "Do you know this John Perry Barlow?" And he said, "Do I know him? He's a co-conspirator." I think he also mentioned to her that I was a Grateful Dead lyricist. He said he thought sending John to the Bar Cross was a good idea, but part of what he was thinking was that having John there would make it easier for him to see Caroline when she came to visit her brother in Wyoming that summer. Which, of course, it did.

So I was sitting at my desk one night when the phone rang, and I picked it up to hear this breathy voice on the phone saying, "Hi. This is Jacqueline Onassis." And I said, "In the highly unlikely event that this isn't a joke, what can I do for you?" And she said, "It isn't a joke. I have something I'd like to discuss with you." A couple of days later, John was on the Bar Cross.

My first impression of him was that he was incredibly good-looking and had a kind of thoughtless grace that was great to see in someone his age. In some respects, John was a lot younger than his years but also had a wise-fool quality in that he was permanently rambunctious but charming as well. He was also exquisitely beautiful but very sweet-natured and funny. Really hilarious. And not full of himself in any way. Not a preppie guy at all.

I stuck him in a bunkhouse that was partially filled with irrigation water, but he was cool with that because it was dry where he was sleeping. The hands on the ranch thought it was funny, but they were all oddities of their own sort. They saw that he was very green indeed, but many of them were also kind of green. I had found that I could hire kids from urban and suburban areas and they would work like hell and not necessarily be good at it at first, and so John fit right in.

John was physically powerful and fearless, and I could put him to anything and he would do it and then do it again when he didn't get it right the first time. He was not a great horseman, but cowboying is not dressage.

He stayed on the ranch for about two and a half months, and his sister, Caroline, came around quite a bit as well. During that summer, John and I took acid together for the first time. He had already taken a little but never as large a dose as three hundred micrograms. He liked it, though, and we had a terrific time together. We went driving because back then what I liked to do when I was tripping was get in my truck and see how far I could go in directions where you weren't supposed to get very far at all.

Another thing John and I did while we were tripping was drop explosives down one of the uncapped gas wells that were all around. I had gleaned from *The Blaster's Handbook* where I could get these canisters made out of plastic that were about two inches in diameter and eight to ten inches long that packed a pretty good charge. I'd prepare the charge with a lit fuse, rather than an electrical one, then I would set it so I could drop the charge down the holes, some of which were four or five miles deep, and it wouldn't go off until the canister itself was at least a mile and a half to two miles down.

When it did go off, the sound that would issue forth from the belly of our earth at this particular kind of tickling was just extraordinary. If anything came flying back out of the hole, it was a sign that I had done something wrong. I either didn't have enough of a fuse on it or I hadn't taken into consideration that there were gas pockets down there. I definitely did not want to start a gas-well fire. That would have been kind of a dead giveaway.

About a year later, in November 1978, there was a big party at Le Club in New York City to celebrate John's eighteenth birthday and Caroline's twenty-first birthday as well as to commemorate the fifteenth anniversary of John Kennedy's assassination. Eddie Hill, who was then John Jr.'s roommate at Andover, came up to me that night and said, "Mr. Barlow, I have to tell you the Grateful Dead are more important to me than my family, my religion, and my school." And I said, "Hey, man, you had better reexamine your priorities."

That night, I got a crash course in what it was like to be a Kennedy in New York City. The paparazzi were everywhere and as people were coming out of the birthday party, there was a fracas when one of John's more jock-y friends from Boston decided he was going to engage in fisticuffs with some irritating guys. The next day, the story was all over the *New York Post* and the *Daily News*.

I first got to spend some significant time with Jacqueline Kennedy Onassis when I drove out to Peapack, New Jersey, to have Thanksgiving dinner with her, a boyfriend candidate, John, Caroline, and my wife, Elaine. It was just us, and Jackie and I hit it off immediately.

At one point after we had gotten to know each other better, I asked her, "What is it like to be so goddamn famous? It must be weird." And she said, "I realized Jack was going to become a big deal, and it took a while for me to understand the consequences that might have on me. Because, as you see, I'm really kind of shy. But I wanted to be with him and if that was the price, I was willing to pay it. I then came to see that people were making a big deal out of me, too. At first, I liked this. But then it made me feel like prey.

"Gradually, I realized that all this stuff in the press really wasn't about me. It was actually a comic strip that had a character in it that looked like me and did some of the things I did but wasn't me. It was something they were making up. And I read it quite avidly for a while, and then I realized that it was making me sick so I stopped."

She was a truly extraordinary human being, and one of her greatest accomplishments was the ability to tear people's gaze away from the Macy's Thanksgiving Day balloon the media had made of her and bring their attention to the person she actually was, who was even more remarkable.

TWENTY

HEAVEN HELP THE FOOL

I was living on the ranch on my own and started bringing out these thoroughbred girls I had known in New York and Los Angeles to keep me company. They would break a fingernail and that would be that: Goodbye, Bar Cross Ranch. Having all these temporary frontier housewives on the ranch wasn't working out very well, and so I finally concluded that it was impossible to operate a large cattle ranch in Wyoming without conceding that a man and a woman had to run it together. That was just the way it had to be. There was a natural division of labor that required two people to fulfill.

I knew I needed a woman who was tough enough for the position, and I thought about all the girls I had ever been romantically involved with. I even went so far as to make another list that included some with whom I had never had a relationship.

I had begun my career in the study of women at Fountain Valley. I was still a virgin then, but I guess you could say that technically I had lost my virginity about a year before I went there. In those days, there were cathouses all along the Union Pacific railroad line. I went down to one in Evanston, Wyoming, with a bunch of my miscreant friends and that was that, but I never thought of it as being the real thing. I later learned that Daniel Ellsberg had lost his virginity in the same kind of cathouse in Laramie.

Toward the end of my sophomore year, I fell into a high school romance with a "townie" in Colorado Springs. I had gone into the city one afternoon with some friends and we were just killing time when I met Judy on a bus. In our way, we loved each other an awful lot. Both of us were still really virgins, and so we went at the process of crossing that divide together. I was sixteen at the time and she was a very heated-up Southern Baptist, which lent a certain something to it all.

I spent the summer after I graduated from Fountain Valley working in Colorado Springs as an independent contractor for the sale of frozen confectionaries. In other words, I drove a Popsicle truck. It was a little pink Jeep with a surrey roof and a small mechanical music box that played the same hugely and poorly amplified lullaby about every eleven seconds all day long. Sometimes that song still comes back to me in a dream. Most of the time, extreme rendition could not force me to repeat it.

As a marketing aid, I was wearing chaps and a cowboy hat, and I would show up wherever I pleased so I could constantly surprise the kids. I always wanted to work in the sections of town where the families did not have enough money to afford a big refrigerator but could afford Popsicles, especially as they were being sold by a mythological fellow like me. That summer, I made serious bank.

One day I was driving past the front yard of the house of Judy's best friend, Elaine Parker. She was out working on her tan, and it was working. Elaine had dark eyes and dark hair and the kind of skin that could really take a tan. She asked me in for some lemonade and from that day forward, I knew one thing about Elaine Parker and me. We were good at that.

Nonetheless, I did my best to keep my relationship with Judy alive during my freshman year at Wesleyan. There were several weekends when I drove from Middletown to Colorado Springs to see her. It was about 1,900 miles each way and I would leave on Friday and come back on Sunday. My metallic purple 1965 Chevy Impala Super Sport had a 550-horsepower engine that I had souped up by putting two four-barrel carburetors in it. I had fucked with this car so significantly that I could run it for hours at insane speed.

Gas cost only twenty-eight cents a gallon back then, but I was not getting even ten miles to the gallon at the speed I was driving. I almost had to stand under the hood while constantly pouring gas right into the carburetors to keep going. Back then, the speed limit was eighty-five miles an hour, but no one seemed all that concerned about enforcing it and so I would be going a hundred miles an hour easy.

At about three o'clock one Kansas morning while I was going roughly 130 miles an hour and had been for a long time, I was not quite nowhere but I could certainly see it. Suddenly, the main bearings in the differential seized and the rear wheels were locked. With astonishing velocity, I veered off the highway into a cornfield. Entering a cornfield at 130 miles an hour is like slamming into deep water. Breathtaking.

After the car finally came to a dead stop, I walked back up to the highway and stood by the side of the road until someone came along and picked me up. While I was standing there, I suddenly realized that driving all the way to Colorado Springs to spend the night with my girlfriend was even crazier than I was. I couldn't do it anymore.

Instead, I decided to focus my attention on the women's colleges of New England, and I discovered that I could ride my motorcycle to places like Bennington and Sarah Lawrence, recite poetry of my own composition to anyone who might be interested, and do okay without a 1,900-mile booty call.

Between April 1966 and December 1974, I was involved with many other women, but I never lost contact with Elaine. At one point, she was operating the cash register at the Yale Law School cafeteria, and I went to see her there. But just when I thought that we might start something up, she fell in with a promising student there who then became, at a startlingly young age, the president of the Union Pacific railroad. They were together for several years, and he took her with him to southern California.

Elaine eventually broke up with him and returned to Colorado

Springs, where she got into a relationship with a guy we had both known when I was at Fountain Valley. For a summer, they traveled around the Rockies in a VW bus with Elaine's older sister, who had fallen in with him, too. Eventually, their road led to the Bar Cross.

Although it was the middle of haying season, Elaine and I felt pretty cozy with each other. The feeling that I had after she left made me understand strongly that, whether we'd had a romantic history or not, she was now at the top of my list. It would still be a long-distance relationship, but I had gotten a pilot's license and was leasing a plane, so I started flying down to Colorado Springs to see her nearly every weekend.

This courting by airborne siege went on for a while until she finally said, "Barlow, what are you doing?" And I said, "I am attempting to win your heart." And she said, "Keep working on it." And I said, "At least, I'd like you to come up and share the Bar Cross Ranch with me for a while."

She said yes, and we lived there together along with my mother from December 1974 until July 1976, at which time Elaine had had a belly full of me and dashed back to Colorado Springs. I spent the balance of that summer engaged in a relationship with a girl who would have been the answer to all of my financial dilemmas. She was also beautiful, smart, and funny, and I might have ended up with her, but I realized that trouble would come between us, as it does to every married couple, and I didn't want there to be a little voice in the back of my head saying "You did it for the money."

By Christmas of that year, neither Elaine nor I was very happy, and I resumed my lonely flights of courtship down to Colorado Springs. Over a period of about a month, I persuaded her to come back. This time, I wanted to nail it out of the chute, and so I proposed to her almost immediately, setting a date and beginning to create a matrix of details and expectations that might keep her from bolting again.

We were to be wed on the Bar Cross on June 21, 1977, the day of the summer solstice. Let me tell you that, as difficult as being married can be, getting ready to be married can be even more difficult still, especially if you're involving hundreds of people who know no master.

Weir was going to be my best man, and we had agreed that, on the day of the wedding, we would go up on the hill at sunrise to lay out a line of rocks pointing away from a big medicine circle we had built. Then at sunset, when we expected the service to be over, everybody would pick up a rock and lay it out pointing to the setting sun.

The night before, everyone was drinking. Earlier in the day, Weir and I had both gone straight to the Everclear, which is pure ethanol, 190 proof. You can run your race car on it. Everclear is not really meant for human consumption, but it is sold in liquor stores. We each had a pint of it in our hip pockets and we weren't mixing it with anything.

At some point during the night, Weir apparently abandoned me and went off to sleep in a bunkhouse. This was an act of disloyalty I could not abide. In those days, it had become my practice to punctuate points I wanted made very clearly by blanging off a round from my .357 Magnum into the floor. Since the bullet leaves the muzzle of that gun at twice the speed of sound, the exclamation point it makes is accompanied by two sonic booms.

At about four-thirty in the morning, I went out to fetch the faithless Weir from his alcohol-induced coma. I entered the bunkhouse and, without any warning, I fired off my exclamatory round into the floor. But I had forgotten that this was the only inhabited building on the ranch that didn't have a plank floor. In fact, it had once been a chicken coop and had a concrete floor, over which we had placed a rug.

There was a remarkable silence as there often was following one of these shots across the bow. Suddenly, Weir said, "You shot me!" And I said, "Oh, I did not." He said, "Turn on the light. Come see." I turned on the lights and went over to him and sure as shit, it was clear that I had shot him. It was a minor wound but a piece of shrapnel had gone all the way through Bobby's nose, and in fact the entire wall right above his bed was peppered with shrapnel.

If Bobby had sat up when I had come through the door, I would have killed him for sure. Which would have given the day an entirely different flavor. But what it came down to instead was that Weir wound up serving as my best man with a Band-Aid over his nose.

Right after this incident, I jumped on my motorcycle and left the ranch. In the tradition of the groom not seeing the bride before the wedding, Elaine was staying with a close friend of mine. I don't think I mentioned the shooting when I came to see them that night, but after I had left the ranch, the guests talked about whether or not to follow me. The first question anyone asked was, "Is he still armed?"

The next day, a wonderful man performed the ceremony, the Reverend Calvin Elliot, who had grown up next door to Katharine Hepburn in the tonier end of Hartford, Connecticut, back in the days when Hartford had a tony end. The reverend had come to Wyoming because he felt closer to God there. He was conservative but extremely refined and a real gentleman. In the sunset light, he looked like God almighty. There was a party after the wedding, and John and Caroline Kennedy were both there because John was still working for me at that point.

Elaine and I had talked about a honeymoon but had not gotten up a serious plan. Although Weir had been muttering about me going with him to Los Angeles for a while to keep working on the album that came to be called *Heaven Help the Fool*, I didn't realize that none of the songs had been written yet and we were already paying for studio time. Unfortunately for me, by shooting Weir on the night before the wedding, I had significantly lengthened his guilt lever.

We'd already had one emergency songwriting session in Salt Lake City. I was drinking and doing cocaine with him and we went to see the Mormon Tabernacle Choir while more or less stinking drunk. We were staying in the Hotel Utah, where my parents had gotten married, because Weir and I thought that if we got together in a hotel room, it would help us work. We got Keith Olsen, who had just produced the Dead's *Terrapin Station*, to come out as well. As far as I could tell, his principal function seemed to be supplying us with blow.

Weir went to Los Angeles right after the wedding, and then I followed him out there five days later. I left Elaine behind, which was not a terribly romantic thing to do, but nevertheless that was what happened. And so Elaine and I never did have a honeymoon. She took that period of time to move into the main house on the ranch, which she felt was fair to claim as hers.

After the wedding, my mother had gone off on an extended tour of the South Pacific and was then in Papua New Guinea among the mud men. Which meant that, among other things, Elaine was able to remove the Christmas tree that had been in the living room for more than eleven years. It was a gigantic sagebrush, seven feet tall and nine feet wide, the likes of which you rarely see. My mother had put twenty-eight hundred little white Italian lights on it, which had been quite an ordeal for me to watch her do. Why did she do this? Because it was an objet d'art. That was what my mother said all of her artist friends called it. Elaine felt like she now had the right to take that damn tree down, and I was totally with her on that.

In Los Angeles, I wrote the lyrics for six of the eight tracks on *Heaven Help the Fool* in a short time, pretty much the whole album. I'm still proud of that record because I think it turned out amazingly well. Weir was playing with some truly serious studio musicians, including David Paich, Mike Porcaro, Bill Champlin, David Foster, Nigel Olsson, Waddy Wachtel, and Tom Scott. Generally, they were right there in the room playing alongside Bobby. It was definitely a scene of major proportions, but if you're not a musician, the studio can really be a dreadful place because nothing happens for the longest time.

I returned to the ranch to find a whole new order in place. Which was okay by me. It had to happen sooner or later, and I was glad to see Elaine becoming the woman of the Bar Cross.

TWENTY-ONE

ADULT BEHAVIOR

On October 2, 1977, I had the forehead-slapping realization that I was about to become an age above which nobody could be trusted. In fact, I'm still not sure that it makes good sense to trust people over thirty. While I had no aspirations to become a grown-up—and I think we all know what that is—I did want to be an adult who was regarded as responsible. I could no longer excuse my peccadilloes on the basis of youth. They had fallen into a less pleasant category, like bad manners.

I went to bed on the eve of my thirtieth birthday only to realize all this, and so I got back up and spent the balance of the night composing a list of advisories to myself that I called "Principles of Adult Behavior." Most of them were blandly inarguable, the sort of platitudes that Polonius had laid on Hamlet. Because I advocated avoiding the pursuit of happiness, this particular homily served to actively piss off the broadest range of folks you could imagine.

Over the course of the ensuing years, I have done my best to keep the list posted wherever I am. And so I am going to include it here:

1. Be patient. No matter what.

2. Don't bad-mouth: Assign responsibility, not blame. Say nothing of another you wouldn't say to him.

3. Never assume the motives of others are, to them, less noble than yours are to you.

4. Expand your sense of the possible.

5. Don't trouble yourself with matters you truly cannot change.

6. Expect no more of anyone than you can deliver yourself.

7. Tolerate ambiguity.

8. Laugh at yourself frequently.

9. Concern yourself with what is right rather than who is right.

10. Never forget that, no matter how certain, you might be wrong.

11. Give up blood sports.

12. Remember that your life belongs to others as well. Don't risk it frivolously.

13. Never lie to anyone for any reason. (Lies of omission are sometimes exempt.)

14. Learn the needs of those around you and respect them.

15. Avoid the pursuit of happiness. Seek to define your mission and pursue that.

16. Reduce your use of the first personal pronoun.

17. Praise at least as often as you disparage.

18. Admit your errors freely and soon.

19. Become less suspicious of joy.

20. Understand humility.

21. Remember that love forgives everything.

22. Foster dignity.

23. Live memorably.

24. Love yourself.

25. Endure.

I don't expect the perfect attainment of these principles. However, I post them as a standard for my conduct as an adult. Should any of my friends or colleagues catch me violating any one of them, bust me.

John Perry Barlow, October 3, 1977

I showed this list to Jerry Garcia a few weeks later and he said, "I hope your embarrassment insurance policy is paid up."

TWENTY-TWO

ÉMINENCE GRISE

O n purely genetic grounds, I was always considered to be a Republican in Wyoming and had worked for several years as a precinct captain in Sublette County. In 1978, I was elected as the chairman of the Republican Party in Sublette County, and I went to the Republican state convention in June.

Alan Simpson, an old family friend who was about to be elected to the U.S. Senate from Wyoming, said, "I've got a guy here I want you to meet and consider working for. I don't think you're going to like him because he's too smart by half. But Dick Cheney does know how to deal with the federal government. He can play fuck 'em with anybody in Washington, D.C., and he cares just as much about protecting Wyoming as you do."

That was precisely what I wanted in a state where 78 percent of the land was controlled by the federal government, which meant that somebody other than the people who lived there were in charge and rarely making decisions that anybody there agreed with.

I met with Cheney, and I wasn't predisposed to like him on the strength of what Alan Simpson had said but I was prepared to swallow it and act like I did. He knew who I was, but I think he treated everyone like they were less than him, and in some respects, they were. Dick Cheney is one of the two smartest men I've ever met, the other being Bill Gates. He could take you on a devastatingly rapid tour of all the weak points in your arguments. That didn't mean he was right, but it sure meant that he could show you where you were wrong.

After having served as Gerald Ford's chief of staff in the White House, Cheney had run Ford's unsuccessful 1976 presidential campaign. In great part, Dick's motivation in running for Congress from Wyoming was his desire for legitimacy.

As is almost always the case in Wyoming, that particular election was decided in the Republican primary. I began working for him as his western Wyoming campaign coordinator with some enthusiasm because he seemed like a crisp unit and I could see launching him on Washington and getting everything we wanted. Having already been the éminence grise for the better part of the Ford administration, Dick would have a hell of a lot more standing in Congress than any other freshman representative from Wyoming, and therefore be able to do more for us in Washington than anyone else ever had. To be honest, I didn't do a great deal for him during that campaign, but that was partly because it was haying season on the ranch.

After Dick got elected, he was a fierce advocate for Wyoming, and we worked together on a lot of issues, both at home and in D.C. At the time, I was president of the Wyoming Outdoor Council, the largest homegrown conservation group in the state. We were not a preservation group; rather, we believed there were many uses of the federal ecosystem that could be accessed by humans without diminishing their biological integrity. But we did not wish to be trapped in the long-running battle between the urban professional class and the rural working class, which is far too often where environmental battles get disputed.

I'd actually first gotten involved in all this when I returned to Wyoming in 1971. At the time, the El Paso Natural Gas Company and the U.S. Atomic Energy Commission had come up with the bright idea of

blowing up five separate 100-kiloton nuclear devices right below Pinedale so they could shatter the entire Pinedale Anticline formation and
then begin doing wide-scale fracking there.

I helped stop this with some cowboy theater. Floyd Bousman, a
central-casting rancher as well as a man of great probity, and I went
on the *Today* show together, and we basically just deep-sixed the entire plan. There was a whole community effort behind stopping it, and
President Richard Nixon promised that if we came to Washington, we
would be given the opportunity to meet with James Schlesinger, who
was then the head of the Atomic Energy Commission.

By the time we got to D.C., Nixon had just made Schlesinger the
secretary of defense, and his replacement at the AEC, Dixy Lee Ray,
refused to meet with us. The truth was that they were scared, and they
had good reason to be because after that project got shut down, there
was no more discussion about the nuclear stimulation of natural gas.

After Dick Cheney took office, our biggest concern was the glut of
new oil production in the Jonah Field down below Pinedale that was
going to release a lot of sulfur dioxide into the atmosphere. We were
diametrically opposed to that because we were already getting about
as much acid rain as we could take, or at least that was how it seemed
to me.

Dick wanted to know why that was, and I explained that there were
three giant copper smelters along the Mexican border. In cooperation
with the Natural Resources Defense Council, we had proven a direct
correlation between production at those smelters and acid rainfall levels
in the mountains. Although the smelters were quite far away, the stuff
would get way up into the atmosphere, and then solar conditions would
turn it all into sulfuric acid. Cheney was appalled to find out this was
happening and got right on board with us. Within a short period of
time, all three plants were shut down. Dick's power in Washington was
that he knew how to get shit done.

Even back then, there was all this prissy bullshit about nature and
what nature wanted. As far as I could tell, nature just wanted to be left
alone as much as possible and otherwise it didn't give a shit. For me,
the most important issue was to vouchsafe the quality of life for the

habitat. That was the only thing I wanted to focus on. I didn't care if you were bait fishing or fly-fishing just as long as you were taking care of the habitat.

As a result I found myself constantly dealing with class warfare by another name. When Congress was about to pass a Wyoming wilderness bill that would have put additional land under federal control, a whole bunch of snowmobilers were distressed by the prospect that they would no longer be allowed to go into what would now be a designated federal wilderness area. So I came up with the bright idea of having an additional category of federal wilderness where people could snowmobile during certain months because all the wildlife would be asleep and the only animals who would actually get disturbed were cross-country skiers. But of course the skiers were very disturbed. That was what I meant by class warfare: The cross-country skiers were mostly young urban professionals, whereas the people who liked to ride snowmobiles were kind of rough and tumble and lower middle class.

In the end, Cheney got my new designation put into effect, but in the process, both the Sierra Club and the Wilderness Society made me into their leading enemy. If you go to the middle of the road, chances are good that you will get run over.

Another ongoing issue at the time was that unscrupulous developers were dividing large chunks of motherless sagebrush into forty-acre tracts without granting a right of way to others. The entire state was rapidly becoming more and more yuppified because all these decisions were being made by the federal government in Washington rather than by locals in Wyoming.

During this period, I watched Wyoming change around me, and so I tried to amplify greatly the idea that what we wanted was "Wyoming on Wyoming's Terms," which had been a founding idea of the Wyoming Outdoor Council. By then, Jackson Hole had started to make Aspen look like a good start. When I was born in Jackson Hole, there had been only one doctor in the entire town.

But it was so beautiful there and you could ski and so it went. I always felt that the guy riding a bucking horse on the state license plate was anyone who was trying to stay on top of Wyoming.

TWENTY-THREE

GLOBAL SOCIOPATH

Dick Cheney wound up spending ten years as Wyoming's only congressman. In 1989, President George H. W. Bush selected Dick to become his secretary of defense. That was when I realized that he was, in fact, a sociopath. It was an opinion I developed during the course of our battles over the MX missile–basing system that Dick did everything in his power to realize.

Unlike the U.S. Navy, the Air Force in the 1980s did not have any missile submarines but still wanted to have their own nuclear retaliatory weapons. It was like the Air Force–Navy football game and so the Air Force scratched its head and came up with the MX, an intercontinental ballistic missile that could carry ten to twelve 300-kiloton nuclear warheads, a little like its submarine-based cousin, the Trident missile, which had eight warheads of 100 kilotons each. To give you some basis for comparison, the nuclear bomb that was dropped on Hiroshima consisted of about 17 kilotons.

One MX could spray the entire Soviet Union with the most vivid kind of hell, and the idea was that they were going to build a thousand apparent MX missile sites, of which only a hundred would house actual MX missiles with nuclear warheads. They were then going to put all these missiles on railroad tracks and shuttle them from tunnel to tunnel and into these little bunkers that were scattered all around Nevada and Utah and southern Oregon and a little part of Wyoming and Arizona. Since there would be absolutely no way for the Russians to know where the real missiles actually were at any given point in time, they would have to figure out a way to destroy them all in order to feel safe about launching a nuclear first strike, which would have been impossible.

To make this happen, the Air Force was going to build railroad tracks all over the intermountain West. To construct the railroad tracks and the tunnels and the bunkers, they were going to use all of the water in the intermountain West. There is large amount of territory between the ridges of the Sierras and the Wasatch Mountains where there is no outlet, and so all the rain and snow that falls there has nowhere to go but down into the Carson Sink or the Humboldt Sink or the Black Rock Desert. This is a completely contained zone and so all the water that lies beneath the earth there is ancient water that is millions and millions of years old. They were going to pump this sacred aquifer dry.

I first got upset about the obvious folly of this from an environmental standpoint. Then I realized, "Jesus Christ, this doesn't make sense anyway." We already had eighteen Trident submarines with twelve missiles on them and each of those had eight warheads and no one could have ever even begun taking them all out. So what the fuck did we need with a hundred fully armed MX missiles as well?

As the father of a brand-new daughter with another on the way, the fact that the U.S. government was trying to come up with a way to make nuclear war seem somehow winnable or plausible or even thinkable was just anathema to me. I got really frantic about it. I started to get more and more engaged in nuclear weapons policy, and oddly enough, it turned out that as secretary of defense, Dick Cheney was now to a large extent the chief architect of American nuclear weapons policy. He was leading the charge to get all this approved in Congress while claiming that it would be good for the economy. In fact, his reasons for doing this were far weirder and much deeper.

I had always gotten along pretty well with Dick on all the other stuff we had argued about. We had been able to come to compromises, because basically we wanted the same thing on a lot of these deals, which was Wyoming on its own terms. But he was totally adamant about the MX missile–basing system and at one point, I found myself having a staged argument about it with him in his office in Washington.

Mary McGrory, a well-known columnist for the *Washington Post* back then, asked if she could come along with me to see Dick because she thought it might be interesting. She did, and Dick and I went at it hammer and tongs in front of her for about an hour and a half. I finally dragged myself out of his office bleeding and punctured in many places and she said, "You know, I've been covering this beat since Franklin D. Roosevelt was president and your man Cheney is the scariest person I've ever seen here." She then wrote a column that basically said just that. Dick did not like this at all, but at that point, we were no longer on the best of terms.

And then it got even worse. My organization, the Wyoming Outdoor Council, filed an environmental impact suit claiming that the federal government had not taken into consideration one of the impacts from the MX missile–basing system, which was nuclear war. I thought this was a distinct possibility that no one could ignore. I mean, we were talking real environmental impact now.

I filed that suit on behalf of the organization, and the judge threw it out of court. In his view, the suit was spurious because we were not going to have a nuclear war. My question then was why even bother to build the goddamn thing if you were not going to have a nuclear war?

After that Dick called me up and said, "John Perry, you don't have to worry about the MX-basing scheme anymore." And I said, "Really? Why? Did you cancel the weapons systems?" And he said, "No, no. We're going to go ahead and build them."

By then, though, this weapons system had become pretty controversial even within the Bush administration. People like Brent Scowcroft, who was Bush's national security adviser, didn't like it, and so the tide had started to turn against Dick. I said, "So how are you going to base them?" And he said, "We're going to put them in Minuteman silos."

I said, "But wait, you put them in a Minuteman silo and they're like a sitting duck. I mean, you might as well line them up in Red Square. They're completely vulnerable to being totally taken out."

And he said, "Not the way we're going to do it. We're going to put them on launch on warning." That meant that as soon as there was a plausible *warning* of a nuclear first strike, the birds would go. As it happened, all the Minuteman sites were in Wyoming.

I said, "Did you ever see *Dr. Strangelove*?" And he said, "I don't think that's amusing." And I said, "I wasn't trying to be amusing."

It took me years before I realized what Dick was actually up to, which was scaring the living shit out of the Soviets. Because once we started doing stuff like that, there was no telling what else we might do. In a way, Dick was adopting a system I had used back when I was driving in Mexico and there would be one paved strip down the middle of the road. I'd be driving on it and a bus would be coming right at me. The bus driver wanted to stay on that paved strip because the shoulders of the road were not nearly as reliable. I never wanted to get over either but playing chicken with a Mexican bus driver was not entirely a good idea.

I found that if I started weaving all over the road like I was *muy borracho,* the bus driver would pull over, and that was exactly what Dick Cheney was now doing. He was acting like he was completely out of his mind to get the Russians to pull over. Once Dick told me what he was going to do with the MX missiles, that was pretty much it for the two of us.

When Dick became the vice president of the United States under George W. Bush in 2001, all this provided the context for what he wanted to do in the Iraq War, which was pretty much his idea. Bear in mind that this was not a guy who had "feelings" in the usual sense of the word. Dick was motivated by what he considered to be the greater good, but for him the greater good did not have individual faces. It was far more generalized.

Dick thought that the only time the existence of a single world power like the United States had ever worked before was during the Roman Empire. And that was largely because the Romans had done stuff like using roadside crucifixions for decorations, which had served to keep certain kinds of enthusiasm from developing among the people.

This was what Dick really believed, but he hadn't studied the religious aspects of the situation in Iraq and was completely stupid about the Sunnis and the Shiites. Dick was not a spiritual guy at all, so he couldn't understand spiritualism in other people. But I think he really believed that if the United States dove into the Middle East and did something that was wildly irrational and crazy—like attacking a country that had not done us any harm at all—it was going to make everyone else in the world extremely wary of ever messing with us.

That the Iraq War might also have been good for Halliburton, the multinational oil corporation where Dick had served as CEO, is a common way of explaining his behavior in this situation. Never for a minute did I feel that he was motivated by that. Dick was motivated only by power.

Oddly enough, what I admired most about Dick was his ability to fly-fish. He was one of the most beautiful fly fishermen I have ever seen. Honest to God. Dick Cheney would go out on the New Fork River as it flowed through my ranch and toss out these impossibly long fly casts. Watching them snake through the air and then land precisely where he wanted them to go was poetic. He was absolutely an artist with a fly rod.

Apparently, Dick was a lot better at that than he was with a shotgun. But I also think he got a bad rap for shooting his friend in the face. Hell, that sort of thing can happen to goddamn near anyone. Just ask Bobby Weir.

TWENTY-FOUR

FEEL LIKE A STRANGER

The Grateful Dead started working on *Go to Heaven* in July 1979 but did not release the album until January of the next year. They were doing overdubs like madmen, and although I lost faith in the project, I did write lyrics and, in some cases, the melody line, to four of the songs, three with Bobby and one with Brent Mydland, who had joined the band in April 1979, after Keith and Donna Godchaux had decided to go out on their own.

One of the songs I wrote with Bobby was "Feel Like a Stranger." The two of us had gone to see Huey Lewis in a club called Uncle Charlie's in Corte Madera. The place was kind of a singles scene, and Bobby got the idea that he wanted to write a song about going out and getting laid. Despite the tall horse I was then on about Weir's moral imperfections, I wasn't exactly opposed to that concept myself.

The real problem was that Bobby wanted me to put all these low-falutin' ideas into the song. We were having what rapidly became a seriously overheated discussion about it in Bobby's house in Mill Valley. He didn't like the lyrics I was coming up with because, as I recall, they were too "poetic." And so I said to him, "If there's one literate man left in America, then I'm writing for him."

A gay guy who was Bobby's friend was staying with him at the time. The guy was trying to sleep on the couch when our argument got totally out of hand and Weir ran upstairs and locked himself in the bathroom. I followed him up there and kicked my way through the door, and that was when we started throwing punches at each other.

It was the first and last fight we ever had, and I'm sure I would have been much less likely to attack him if I hadn't been drunk. Can either of us fight? Generally not well and certainly not when we don't want to hurt each other. Although I had been in bar fights, Weir may have never been in a fight before in his life. He was in a fight with me that night only because I was fighting him.

After silence had settled on the scene the next morning, I came back downstairs, and Bobby's friend was sitting up on the couch. I could only imagine how wide open his eyes must have been the night before because of the totally erotic nature of the event that had taken place upstairs. "I didn't know what I was going to do with you boys last night," he said. "I was afraid I was going to have to spray a garden hose on you or something."

My marriage to Elaine had many difficulties. One of them, as might already be evident, was that I was an alcoholic. I was not drinking every day. Like my father and like most ranchers and cowboys in Wyoming, I was a binge drinker. I would drink steadily for two or three days at a time. Although I would still be functional while I was drinking, Elaine became a full-on codependent, which I believe can be a worse affliction than alcoholism.

If you are an alcoholic, everybody says, "Oh, all you need is will-power. Pull yourself up and be a man and stop drinking." But what they say about your wife is, "I don't know how she does it. She's a saint. She's fantastic. How does she put up with him?" In truth, we were both into it up to our eyeballs.

Despite that, we were actually pretty happy until we began having children. I had reached a point where I was so determined to have kids that if we weren't going to have them, I wasn't sure I wanted to be married anymore. Partly because of my alcoholism and partly because the financial situation on the ranch was always precarious, Elaine was never sure about having kids.

As it turned out, Elaine gave birth to three daughters in six years, the first in 1982. I don't know why but for some reason, Elaine and I were both convinced that our first child would be a boy. We hadn't had an amniocentesis or anything like that done because we weren't particularly interested in finding out what sex our child was until it happened. Our nickname for the baby was Bingo.

Our first daughter was actually goddamn near born on the road between Pinedale and Jackson Hole, which is a distance of about seventy miles. Elaine's water broke and she went into labor and I was driving like Neal Cassady and just barely got to the hospital in time. At one point, it seemed that I was going to deliver the child myself in the parking lot.

We hadn't prepared any names for a girl, and all of sudden we had to come up with one. I wanted to call her Liberty, and Elaine wanted to call her Jessica. So as you can see, the bargaining gap was not exactly small. Elaine finally accepted Leah as the name because in the Bible, Leah is a virtuous person who takes the rap for the wicked Rachel. I thought it would be good to give her a first name that would go with being a virtuous person and then back it up with a middle name that was not so virtuous. I picked her second name from the title of the first book of Lawrence Durrell's Alexandria Quartet. In fact, I named her after both Durrell's Justine and the Marquis de Sade's Justine.

The fact that Elaine would choose Jessica as our daughter's name and that I wanted to call her Liberty made it clear to me that, aside from being sexually crazy for each other, we really did not have all that much in common. It was a lot like my mother and father's marriage.

Despite all that, Leah Justine was joined by Anna Winter in 1984 and then by Amelia Rose in 1986. We were living on the ranch so there were always other people around, but our three daughters took up most of Elaine's time. She was and is absolutely the best mother in the world, but as the fire between us cooled after the girls were born, I started to feel restless at home. And like my father I began to look elsewhere.

Even though I was not completely faithful to Elaine during this period, it was always my strong intention to stay married to her. So I made sure that whatever I did was a one-night stand that would not come back to affect our marriage.

TWENTY-FIVE

WORD PROCESSING

I knew nothing at all about computers until I bought a word processor in 1985. I had started writing screenplays so I could keep the ranch afloat, though I never had any intention of getting any of them made. In those days, the Hollywood studios were paying good money to have screenplays written so they could then retire the intellectual property. So I ended up writing four or five, and I was able to sell them for twenty or thirty thousand dollars each. This is rather ironic considering my subsequent feelings with regard to copyright.

Even though I saw screenplays as something easy I could do for cash, I was dedicated enough to quality that if I felt like I really had to make a change in a script, I would do it. This was no easy process. I was working on a typewriter, and making a change somewhere in the middle of a screenplay meant having to retype about forty pages of the goddamn thing, which made me feel completely and tragically overwhelmed.

I kept thinking, *Screenwriters have been doing it like this all along? How did they not all blow their brains out?* Then I ran across somebody who said, "We now have this thing called a word processor that will allow you to make corrections as you go." And I said, "I will now have this thing as well." I think the first one I ever bought was a Compaq luggable that weighed about thirty pounds.

Around that time I was approached by a crazy, powerful, and mean movie producer named Ray Stark, who had produced *Funny Girl, The Way We Were, The Sunshine Boys,* and *The Electric Horseman.* He was quite the old monster from way back in Hollywood, the kind of dragon who comes out from underneath the hill every hundred years and is not pleased by how things are going.

Ray offered me and a big-time Hollywood television producer named Philip DeGuere the gig of writing a magical realistic musical about Neal Cassady on the road in America. Phil was a serious Deadhead who had helped film the 1972 show that was eventually released as *Sunshine Daydream.* A lot of the time, I didn't like him all that much. He often manifested aspects of human nature that set off my squeamishness, and even worse, behaviors that I was only too susceptible to myself.

But the Dead said they really wanted this movie to happen and were going to give us their music to use in it. So Phil and I started working on this screenplay together and actually had a good time doing it. He would write a scene and I would write either the scene before or after it and then we'd see whether they fit together at all. The working title was "Asking What for Across the Morning Sky."

When we finished the script, the Dead decided that they didn't want to have any of their songs in it after all. Or, as Jerry Garcia said to me at the time, "This is why we call the Grateful Dead the storehouse of broken dreams."

My career as a screenwriter went on for some months after that, but it was a really hard time in the cattle business, and the ranch was in absolutely hemorrhagic financial morbidity. I had never thought I could keep it going forever and didn't want to be forced to sell it on the courthouse steps. So even though I had been offered a lot more for it in the past, I wound up selling the ranch in 1987 for $1.5 million.

The two guys who bought it were Alejandro Orfila, the former head of the Organization of American States and someone entirely comfortable with the ruling junta in Argentina, and Marshall Coyne, who owned the Madison Hotel in Washington, D.C. I told them both that they couldn't ranch the Bar Cross as sort of a plaything. It would be like buying a real spirited stud horse and expecting to ride him three times a year and not have him act like a bronco when you did.

No one could manage a ranch like that from a distance, because it was a very hands-on proposition. So I agreed to run it for them for another year, and that was when I finally got to fix up everything that needed to be repaired. It was kind of a wonderful gig because I had spent so many years thinking about doing just that without having ever been able to afford it.

As a functioning business, the Bar Cross was entirely valueless and so I thought these guys were going to take a bath on the deal. Between the interest payments and all the improvements, they put a hell of a lot of money into the ranch. I never thought they would get it back. Then, in 2012, the Bar Cross was offered for sale for about $22 million. Just recently, it went back on the block for $38 million and someone snapped it up.

In 1988, Elaine and the girls and I moved off the ranch into a house in Pinedale. Once we did, I suddenly realized that most of the people now living in the valley were worth huge amounts of money. A whole new class of people had made a lifestyle choice and were coming into Sublette County in business jets. They didn't give a shit how much money they made from their ranches because they saw them as fishing holes where they could build a $10 million house and have all their fancy friends out in the summer.

At the time, I had no idea what I was going to do to earn a living. Fortunately, the Grateful Dead finally produced a studio album, *In the Dark*, for which they actually knew the songs. Previously, Grateful Dead songs had been like infant marsupials that had to be protected in the pouch that formed between the band and the Deadheads during the three or four years it took for them to become real songs.

From the time of *Go to Heaven* the band had been too messed up to get into a studio and record an album. But now, they were suddenly all bright-eyed and in possession of a whole album's worth of songs that were fully ready for life outside the pouch. I wrote three songs on that album: "Hell in a Bucket," "Throwing Stones," and "My Brother Esau."

As a consequence of the commercial viability of *In the Dark*, the Grateful Dead were suddenly being asked to fill fifty-thousand-seat stadiums instead of the five-to-eight-thousand-seat venues they had played before. And it occurred to me that now, seemingly overnight, the band was making money like real rock stars, whereas Robert Hunter and I were still scuttling along the bottom of the royalties stack.

So we went to the band and said, "You know, it's a drag for us that what you're putting out there is water from our wells." Their response was kind of a forehead slap: "Jeez, yeah, you're right! We see your point and we'll start paying you both a songwriting retainer." They agreed to pay us a regular fee, and I think I began getting six grand a month from them. This allowed me to be completely experimental about what I was going to do next in my life.

And then, as a result of a commitment Bobby Weir had made for us both that I knew nothing about, I staggered into the computer industry.

P. W. Jenkins
President.

The Little Red Bull himself, president of the Wyoming State Senate, 1927. *Wyoming State Historical Society*

The Barlow family Christmas card, circa 1954.

THE BARLOWS

NORMAN   JOHN PERRY   MIRIAM

Me and Charlie, who was named champion Fat Steer at the Sublette County Fair.

Smoking a joint on the football field at Wesleyan before I deliver a very earnest speech during an anti-war demonstration. The photo then appeared in the *Wesleyan Argus* but wasn't news to anyone. *Andy Leonard*

Hanging out with the very elegant Jon McIntire at the Hotel Navarro in Manhattan during a Grateful Dead tour. *Andy Leonard*

Wearing leather pants in an apartment in New Haven during my days as a drug dealer in New York City. *Andy Leonard*

Bobby and I outside his house in Mill Valley. My back is to the camera and I'm holding a Smith and Wesson Model 19. *Andy Leonard*

I think this picture really captures me. That hat actually hung on the ceiling of the Cora Store for years before it was moved along with a bunch of others to the Wyoming State Historical Society. *Courtesy of Elaine Barlow*

JFK Jr. and yours truly at the Green River Rendezvous celebration in July 1977 while he was working for me on the Bar Cross.

Elaine and I on our wedding night on top of the hill where we were married on the Bar Cross. *John Byrne Cooke*

We were all supposed to come to a New Year's Eve concert in San Francisco by String Cheese Incident dressed as superheroes. Since he always wins, I couldn't think of a more effective one than "The Angel of Death." But he is an amiable sort.
C. Taylor Crothers

Standing at the Finn Place with a 3840 Winchester repeating rifle and a MacIntosh (which was not nearly as powerful). It was twenty degrees below zero, and the photo was taken for a story in the *New York Sunday Times Magazine* about the Electronic Frontier Foundation. *Ted Wood*

Cynthia and I at the Canadian consulate in New York City about two weeks before she died.

Me and the Barlowettes about one third of the way up Denali, which was as far as we got by helicopter. The pilot took the photo.

Bobby and I on the radio in Jackson Hole after having done some drinking together. (May I say in parentheses just how much I still love him after all these years.)
Jay Blakesberg

Backstage in Berkeley with my adviser and deep friend Gilberto Gil, who is pretty damned close to being perfect.
Katherine Armer

Super savvy tech investor Esther Dyson and I try to convince Bill Gates that the Internet is actually greater than the sum of Microsoft's parts. *Getty Images*

Me, more or less the way I have looked for a while. *Bart Nagel*

TWENTY-SIX

WELCOME TO APPLE

In 1987, I was staying with Weir in Mill Valley and writing songs with him when he said, "Oh, by the way, we're going down to Cupertino tomorrow to give a lecture to the people at Apple about using Macintoshes for songwriting." Although Steve Jobs was already gone by then, he had given the Dead all these Macintosh computers that Apple thought were being used for songwriting and other creative purposes. The Dead were actually using them semi-creatively—for accounting in the office.

I said to Bobby, "That's ludicrous. What are we going to say? We don't write songs with a Macintosh. The last time I looked, I write songs with a legal pad and you write them with a guitar." Weir said, "Yeah, but you can bullshit your way through anything and I'll just follow your lead." He had a point. And since I had been around people who used Macintoshes, I figured I could talk a pretty good game.

We drove down the next day, and everybody was sitting in this big auditorium. Once I got up in front of the room, I realized the audience was full of Deadheads. It is bad for your karma to lie to a Deadhead, especially if you are part of their pantheon. They are hapless and completely credulous and will believe anything you tell them. Lying to them about this would have been like drowning puppies.

So I said, "The truth is that I don't write songs with a Macintosh. To the extent that I write songs with a computer at all, I write them with a Compaq luggable, and that's because it seems like a better form of Wite-Out." They were hissing and booing but it was pretty mild, the same kind of reaction I had seen when Weir would forget an entire stanza of a song onstage.

Then I said, "I *would* use a Macintosh but nobody ever told me you had given them to the band." Typical Grateful Dead efficiency. They had them, but nobody had ever made me aware of this. Furthermore, I wasn't actually sure I wanted one because they seemed toylike and promiscuous, so overly user-friendly that it was like they were giving you sloppy wet kisses. To me, the Macintosh really felt like a slut. And, that aside, they were also glacially slow in comparison to the Compaq.

I had the idea that what I wanted at this stage in my career was a device that would put words on paper that looked more or less like what used to come from a Selectric typewriter. As far as I could tell, the best way to do that was by using an IBM. Nonetheless, Bobby and I did the talk, and everyone seemed to like it all right and that was that.

A couple of weeks down the line, I got a letter from somebody at Apple saying they would be happy to provide me with a Macintosh as well as all the fixings, which in those days weren't much. I was supposed to use it and tell them what I thought of it. As it turned out, though, Apple did not send me a Macintosh right away. In fact, they took so long to do so that I started sending them letters asking when it was coming.

Because I knew this big toy was on the way, I started thinking about the Macintosh and obsessing about everybody else's Macintosh. Every time I got around one, I would be fucking with it and screwing it up and then leaving it in a wreck. It was really fun for me to be able to get into the operating system and fool around with it. It turned out that I was, in fact, a computer nerd.

. . .

As I was contemplating the end of my time on the Bar Cross, I began to wonder what was going to happen to the idea of community in the absence of little agricultural towns such as Pinedale, which contained in them a spiritual nutrient that was like the sourdough starter for society. I looked out at television land and the suburbs and I saw little of the sense of shared adversity, willingness to accept differences without suspicion or rancor, or general capacity for samaritanism that had been lovingly commented on by Tocqueville and other early observers of budding American culture.

It dawned on me that one of the substrates that might become the foundation of a new community was the strange and mysterious culture of the Deadheads. But they didn't seem to have a central gathering place that was reliable. They also didn't seem to have the ability to talk casually about community affairs among themselves. And they had no economic focus. At least not until they all became lawyers.

But I found it difficult to study the Deadheads in person. Whenever I tried do so, I found I was up against the sociological equivalent of Heisenberg's uncertainty principle: As I would go roaming through the parking lot before a show, the Deadheads would eventually figure out who I was and then begin asking me questions, which meant that my ability to observe them objectively was gone because they were now behaving differently in my presence.

My friend Betsy Cohen, who was then at the Center for Computer Research in Music and Acoustics at Stanford, said, "One way you could study them would be on the Internet." I said, "What's the Internet?" She then explained to me what that was, taking a quantity of time and language that embarrasses me to contemplate today.

At the end of her explanation, I still wasn't quite sure what it was. But she helped me get a 300 baud modem complete with a rubber suction cup to attach to my phone receiver (for which I would have paid a considerable fine, had it been discovered, because it was an alteration of AT&T equipment). In addition, she got me a Tymnet dial-up number and an Internet address through Stanford. After that, I was on my own.

It was assumed that people who had modems with rubber suction cups knew all about the AT command set that one needed to operate modems. I had to learn how to do this the hard way because back then nobody else in Sublette County, Wyoming, even had a modem. I would be dialing the Tymnet number and eventually one sacred day, I heard the strange, seductive warble and boop that means you have connected to modems.

I immediately tried to log in my Stanford address and lo, I was on the Internet. I then followed Betsy's instructions to get myself to the vast terrain of Grateful Dead–oriented Usenet groups where I could see people at all hours of the day or night rendering judgment about me and my closest friends in a condition that was entirely innocent. But it did suffice to teach me a lot about the culture of the Deadheads.

What was much more interesting to me was the Internet itself. Immediately, it became clear to me that this was the nervous system of the noosphere—a postulated sphere dominated by consciousness and the mind and interpersonal relationships—that I had been thinking about ever since I first encountered the notion in the works of Father Pierre Teilhard de Chardin while in college.

Teilhard de Chardin was a Jesuit renaissance man and a world-class paleontologist. He discovered Peking man and wrote a lot about the idea that the evolutionary process had reached a point of self-awareness and was now occupying a new layer of the relational ecology, which was the collective organism of mind.

I had spent fifteen years riding around the Bar Cross thinking about the noosphere, and suddenly after all that time, I had evidence that this was not just Teilhard's pipe dream but was in fact real and growing its own nervous system. Indeed, it had been doing so since 1844, when Samuel F. B. Morse had tapped out the first telegraph message—"What hath God wrought?"—in Washington, D.C. Which is earlier than most people think of cyberspace being born. I knew then and there that without any plan or execution, I wanted to be part of making this particular concept happen.

It was about that time that I discovered the WELL, the Whole Earth 'Lectronic Link, which had been founded in 1985 by Stewart

Brand, Larry Brilliant, and Kevin Kelly. Though not connected to the Internet, the WELL was still a fabulous digital salon filled with people who knew about Teilhard de Chardin and who were Deadheads and so open to all forms of wild inquiry. And it was also just about the right size for a small town to be.

All this gave me the ability to see what other people had not yet seen, which was that there was a space there and a community of people who identified with that space. I didn't have a name for that space yet, but neither did anybody else. Back then, nobody called it anything. I'm pretty sure I was first person to identify the nature of that community and space and then start trying to write about it in what I suppose you might call a somewhat literate fashion.

I had also begun thinking about Apple as the new foundational corporate form of gathering. It was going to be horizontal rather than vertical, organic rather than mechanical, and very flat in assembly. As I continued writing letters to Apple asking where my computer was, I began including musings about Apple as a company.

In the beginning, there had been basically two steps on the ladder at Apple. You had Steve Jobs and then everybody else, which was why it always took so goddamn long for things to happen there, like them sending me my computer. In any case, they finally said, "Your computer is in the mail, really. And we've been getting such a kick out of your letters that we want to know if you would consider coming out here and writing a people's history of Apple."

It took me a while but I eventually wound up getting a contract to write the book from Viking Press. To initiate the project, I moved to Silicon Valley and spent the summer there with my family with the understanding that Elaine and my daughters would go back to Pinedale in the fall so the girls could go to school.

Within about a month and half of cruising around the valley, I realized I didn't really want to write a book about Apple, because if you don't have anything nice to say, don't say anything. And it was definitely not nice in there. Although John Sculley was running the show at Apple, the melody of the culture that Steve had created still lingered on in so many ways.

At one point, Steve had made everybody at Apple go to est, which stands for Erhard Seminars Training, and take these soul-destroying courses that had been created by Werner Erhard to transform the way in which people interacted with one another. The stated aim of the program was to teach people how to express themselves naturally rather than follow rules, but a lot of those people just became even bigger assholes than they had been before. Can you imagine an entire company that had been turned into est-holes? It was not pretty. I mean, I've dealt with East German border guards who were a lot friendlier than most of the building attendants at Apple.

Something else that made me realize I did not want to write a book about Apple was what they had done to Elmer Baum, the first guy who ever made a loan to Apple. Elmer was a sweet, marvelous guy. His son Allen had been one of Steve Wozniak's high school buddies, and Elmer had provided the initial startup capital to Apple by taking out a $5,000 loan using Steve Jobs's VW microbus as collateral.

Elmer then decided to go to work at Apple, where he became employee number thirty-four. By the time Elmer decided to retire, he was by far the oldest employee there. But Apple had not yet even considered creating a retirement plan, and so instead of taking care of him, they just fired his ass.

I had been given a wonderful house in San Jose, but that was pretty much contingent on my writing a somewhat fulsome book of praise about Apple and not about est and what they had done to Elmer Baum. By then, I had already gotten totally evangelical about the Internet. Having come to the water of Silicon Valley, I was now bathed in the sea of bits.

I decided that what I really wanted to do was write about how I thought the information companies were going to be fundamentally different from industrial companies. And so I transformed the book into an account of this great changing paradigm that I was going to call *Everything We Know Is Wrong*.

. . .

At some point during the period after Weir and I had gone to talk at Apple, I participated in an intervention for Bobby, and we sent him off to a place called Crutcher's Serenity House in St. Helena. By then, just about everybody in the Dead was struggling with drug issues, and Bobby was no exception.

I was family to him, so to speak, so I went up there to spend family week with him. It was quite an interesting place, supported by the longshoremen's union. That was appealing to Bobby because he was always saying, "I'm anything but anonymous and so I can't go to one of those AA places." But he was putting up with this place, and so I decided to go up there myself. It actually got to me because it was full of people who were really looking at themselves for the first time, and this was when I said to myself, "Yeah, he's an alcoholic, but what about you?"

I came to understand that something about my relationship with Elaine had played a big part in my own alcoholism. For the first time, I also began to understand what her role as a codependent had been in my life. This wasn't all that surprising, because I was then at the peak of my "needs a little work" phase in terms of alcohol use. I could have turned a fire plug into a codependent, and somehow, I had just adapted to her emotional expectations.

I called Elaine from Crutcher's and said, "There's a chance that you and I might have to get more distance from each other so I can get more distance from alcohol." She was totally suspicious of this, but I started going to AA meetings anyway. I quit drinking and didn't really take any drugs, with the occasional exception of psychedelics, for about two years.

TWENTY-SEVEN

A LITTLE LIGHT

In 1989, the Dead released *Built to Last*. Although no one knew this at the time, it would be their last studio album. I wrote the lyrics for five songs on the album, four of them with Brent Mydland and just one, "Picasso Moon," with Weir.

Although Bobby and I had not exactly split as songwriters, he had gone off and written a song in March 1988 with the actor Gerrit Graham. I couldn't figure out why Weir had done this, but mostly I thought that it was his form of retribution for my having been unfaithful to him by writing songs with Brent. Bobby knew that I didn't like Gerrit.

The two of them wrote "Victim or the Crime," which is still arguably the worst Grateful Dead song ever. My real problem with it, shared by other members of the band, was that the first line contained the word "junkie." For the life of me, I could not see Bobby singing that while standing onstage next to Jerry. As it turned out, Jerry didn't seem to mind at all, but that was just how he could be.

Did I actually go on the radio to urge Deadheads to write Weir with their objections to this song? I may have done that. I don't really remember, but I think Weir reacted to what I had said by putting his fist through a wall.

Jerry Garcia wasn't the only one who thought it was what he called "an idiot song." During a show one night while the band was doing "Victim or the Crime," their longtime roadie Steve Parish came up to me and said, "How does it feel to be the guy who wrote the worst Grateful Dead song ever?" And I said, "I didn't write this song, Parish. Gerrit Graham did. Talk to him about it." Without saying another word, he just turned around and slunk off.

Over the course of the 1980s, Brent Mydland had become something like the invisible spine of the Dead. I realized this for the first time when I was given the opportunity to experience the onstage mix, and the only person that everyone listened to was Brent. He was a genius piano player who had the best voice in the band. He could sing his ass off and transpose and improvise like a motherfucker, but they were all still treating him like the new guy in the band. They treated him like shit, and it made him feel like shit.

I knew Brent was shooting heroin, and I knew that it was going to take him out just like it eventually would do to Garcia as well. I saw that Brent was going to die unless I could get the Deadheads to really dig him. I thought that would save him. So I decided to get together with Brent full-time and begin writing more songs with him, which turned out to be unbelievably easy and amazingly different from working with Weir.

Brent and I had afternoons where we wrote four or five songs together in his house in Martinez in the East Bay. It absolutely helped that he was a piano player, but I also had complete faith in his ability to take my lyrics and sing them in the melody that I had in mind.

That was what happened on "Just a Little Light," which is about the gloom that seemed to be gathering around Brent and Jerry and everything that was then going on backstage at Dead shows. I wanted people to notice that there was also still a light left in the world. I was writing about what happens to everyone after a while. Like Hunter's line in

"Scarlet Begonias," "Once in a while, you get shown the light / In the strangest of places if you look at it right." Although I wasn't consciously quoting that, it is one of my favorite Hunter lines.

The song I wrote with Brent that I like best is the lullaby "I Will Take You Home." I wrote the whole thing—melody, words, the works—as I was going up the driveway of his house. Then I sat next to him at the piano as he played it for the first time. It was about his daughters and mine and a promise I needed to make for both of us. That whatever happened, we would be there to take them home. Only Brent didn't live to do that.

Writing songs with Brent was the most intimate thing I have ever done with a man. He would go off to do heroin in the bathroom and then come back and sit down on the piano bench. But when he looked at me, his pupils would be wide open. Totally dilated. Usually when someone is smacked out of his head like that, his eyes become pin-wheels. But Brent's would be huge because it was such an emotional experience for him. Brent had a vocabulary of about three hundred words, but when he was connecting with the emotions of a song, he was right on top of it. He was incredible.

I was doing an interview with John Markoff of the *New York Times* for an article about the Internet on July 26, 1990, when he told me that Brent had died. I was in my office in Pinedale and I started to cry. And even though I had anticipated it, I couldn't stop crying for days. I went to the funeral and fully expected to give the eulogy, but Weir insisted on doing it himself. It was okay with me, but it wasn't okay.

The pallbearers consisted of the remaining members of the Grateful Dead and me, and while we were waiting in the pallbearer room, they acted like a basketball team that was doing just great at the half. They were being assholes together. I was not crying because you don't cry around the Grateful Dead. That just ain't done. By then, we had all adopted a level of emotional availability that ran the full gamut between spite and irony. I have subsequently learned not to gainsay anybody's way of dealing with grief. But they definitely had a weird coping mechanism.

Then I got into the limo with Jerry and his girlfriend to go to the cemetery. Talk about a strange ride. I said, "You know I'm probably the only person who's really able to be a Deadhead and be onstage as well. As such, I think I'm going to go out front for a while because it seems safer there."

Garcia looked at me with an expression of colossal melancholy. "I'd do that if I were you," he said. "Don't you think that's exactly what I would do if I could? But that's the last thing I can do." Around the Grateful Dead by then, it had gotten just that dark.

TWENTY-EIGHT

THE IVORY GAVEL

In 1989, I was transitioning out of the ranch and evolving into my next incarnation, and I decided to run for state senate from Sublette County. Part of the reason I did that was because I had this absolutely exquisite ivory gavel that had two gold butts and a gold band around the middle. After my grandfather had created the county, he immediately ran for its senate seat. They gave him the gavel when he became president of the Wyoming senate. When my father became president of the senate, he had the gold band put in the middle of the gavel and had his name and dates inscribed there, leaving the other butt of the gavel blank. It led me to think that I had some kind of destiny to fulfill by getting my own name on there.

It was not a race in the usual sense of the term. President George H. W. Bush had appointed my close friend and political buddy John Turner, who had been the senator from Sublette and Teton counties, as the new director of the U.S. Fish and Wildlife Service. His senate seat was now vacant, and there was to be a caucus of all the precinct captains of Sublette County to appoint his successor.

There were a number of candidates, and I decided I would be one of them. If a freely confessed acidhead was ever going to get elected to the senate in the most conservative place in the non-Islamic world, I knew it would require an awful lot of glad-handing on the part of somebody who was also not afraid to take a drink. Because in Wyoming, that was really de rigueur.

One of the precinct captains at the caucus was a close friend of mine, a marine who had also been a SEAL and had been in combat ops in both Korea and Vietnam. We had spent a lot of time together, and it seemed to me that healing over what had happened in Vietnam had taken place in us. I really thought that we respected each other a lot.

In the middle of the proceeding, though, this little voice inside my head alerted me to the fact that something weird was about to happen. The guy I thought was my friend stood up rapier straight and denounced me as though he was Cicero and I was Catiline. Because of my anti-war position on Vietnam, he said, I was a traitor. People like me had lost that war for America. People like me had turned their backs on people like him.

There were at least fifty people there, and even though he had just given this incredibly denunciatory speech, I still lost by only one vote. I knew the guy they wound up choosing instead of me very well and the last I heard, he was still in the Wyoming senate leading a life little better than incarceration in a maximum security prison. But he was the kind of guy who liked that sort of thing.

When I found out what the results were, I was out in front of the courthouse with my old friend Alan Simpson. Alan looked at me and said, "One vote. That's gotta mean something. That's no accident."

In fact, it was providential as shit. If I had received that vote, so many things that are the great milestones in my life, both good and bad, would never have happened. There would have been no Electronic Frontier Foundation. And I would still be married, I suspect.

TWENTY-NINE

A CALL FROM THE WHITE HOUSE

Harper's Magazine periodically created forums in which they asked a number of wise people to sort out the issues of the day. In what strikes me even now as something close to magic, a pair of *Harper's* staffers named Jack Hitt and Paul Tough had the prescience of mind to convene a forum on freedom of expression and forbidden information on the Internet.

Almost randomly, they asked a number of prolific WELL beings to discuss where we should draw the line in what can be known, and who should draw that line and how. At one point, with my usual idiotic flair, I had said that I could imagine a future in which it would not only be all right but in fact a moral obligation to hack into the White House computer system. *Harper's* printed this quote with my name attached to it on the flyleaf of their December 1989 issue.

Shortly after that, I picked up my phone in Pinedale one day and someone said, "Hello, this is the White House." And I said, "Oh God, I've been waiting for this call." And the guy said, "Why do you say that?" And I said, "Because of that forum that was in *Harper's*." And he said, "It's kind of about that." And I said, "How could it be *kind* of about that?"

He said, "That was how we found out that there was somebody who was basically a member of the Grateful Dead and also a recently retired Republican county chairman. We wouldn't have thought that was possible. So we hoped you might be the person to arrange something we want to have happen."

By this time, I was looking at the phone like it was an object I'd never seen before. It was one of the moments in my life when reality had looped back up on me. I said, "What would you like me to help engineer?" And he said, "We've been trying to figure out how to address global warming, and we think one way to do so would be to get people to plant a lot of trees. We also think that if the president," who was then George H. W. Bush, "and Jerry Garcia could be seen planting a tree together, a lot of people would plant trees."

I said, "I don't know. But I could certainly run it by him."

So I called up Jerry and after I had told him about this, he said, "You mean the president of the United States?" And then he did the Garcia cackle. Ha-ha-ha. Jerry thought it was really funny, but he didn't exactly say no. Instead, he said, "Let me think about it for a couple of hours."

So he did and when he got back to me, he said, "I've been thinking about that picture of Sammy Davis, Jr., hugging Nixon onstage during the 1972 Republican Convention. And how it didn't do either one of them any good."

Jerry was definitely right about that, but I said, "Wait. This could be an opportunity. Because this guy seems willing to do any goddamn thing for us. He could also bring a whole bunch of people to the table that we don't usually get a shot at that I would really like to take a shot at." Jerry said, "But we don't know anything about this." I said, "I kind of do." And then he said, "Then we better have a meeting with them."

The Dead were going to do a gig at RFK Stadium in Washington, D.C., on July 12, 1990, and so I helped arrange a big powwow in the Georgetown Four Seasons Hotel. As it turned out, we got everybody we wanted to be there: the head of the Environmental Protection

Agency, the assistant secretary of agriculture, and the guy in charge of the U.S. Forest Service. I saw this as an opportunity to get whatever we could from them. I didn't have any specific goals in my mind, but I figured we could all put our heads together and come up with something positive.

And then Garcia came in there looking like God with a hangover. He was using at that point, and all of his hair was flung to one side of his head. He was also in an ugly mood and not about to plant a tree with anybody. All these heavy guys in suits took their fair share of abuse from him. He said, "We know how much you know about what we do, but we can't imagine we all know enough about one another for us to do much good together."

So the photo op with Garcia and President Bush never happened. But I had a few other things I thought I would ask for during the meeting. One that stuck was that prior to this point in time, there had been no market for recycled paper. Everybody was throwing tons of paper into recycling bins, but it wasn't actually getting recycled because there wasn't a big enough demand for it to make building a recycling infrastructure worth the trouble.

I brought this to their attention, and although nothing happened until President Bill Clinton finally got around to issuing an executive order about it in 1993, the Government Printing Office began using only recycled paper. Which was a fuck of a lot of paper. So in the final analysis, a few good things came of this meeting. Not the least of which is my own indelibly inscribed memory of Jerry Garcia interacting in a none-too-positive manner with all the Lords of the Public Domain.

THIRTY

PHIBER OPTIK AND ACID PHREAK

I was still working on the book for Viking Press and determined to deliver it to them when I suddenly became part of the story. One of the first things that happened was that I attended a hackers' conference meeting in San Francisco. This was not the dread thing that people think when someone now uses the word *hacker*. At that time, the hackers' conference was a pretty crusty boys' camp of aging graybeards who had done an awful lot to produce the original Internet and personal computer technology and they were very free and open about what they were doing without much skulking around. At that meeting, I met John Gilmore, who had been the fifth person to go to work at Sun Microsystems. John had then founded Cygnus Solutions, a company that made free software available for commercial use, and so had more than enough money to do just about anything he wanted.

By then, I had become deeply immersed in trying to wrap my head around how to make the book less about new corporate forms and more about society and how it was going to be altered as we entered into what came to be known as cyberspace. Because I could see that incredibly profound changes were already taking place.

At the online forum that *Harper's Magazine* had put together in December 1989, the participants included two skate punks whose adopted screen names were entirely ironic—Acid Phreak and Phiber Optik. As I later learned, their real names were Elias Ladopoulos and Mark Abene, and throughout the discussion they were all over everybody with an in-your-face attitude about hacking that I found to be really offensive.

At one point, I said, "I am becoming increasingly irritated at the idea that you guys are exacting vengeance for the sin of openness. You seem to argue that if a system is dumb enough to be open, it's your moral duty to violate it. Does the fact that I've never locked my house—even when I was away for months—mean that someone should come and teach me a good lesson?"

Acid Phreak then asked me where I lived. I gave him exact directions to my house and then said, "Do you really mean to imply what you did with that question? Are you merely a sneak looking for places to violate? You disappoint me, pal. For all your James Dean–on–Silicon rhetoric, you're not a cyberpunk. You're just a punk." He responded by saying that what I had just posted would allow him to get all my credit information as well as a whole lot more.

I then told Phiber Optik that they didn't scare me at all. I was being a standard old poop and they were being standard young poops. If someone took away their modems, I told them, it wouldn't be that different from taking away their skateboards.

As this was somewhat true, Optik immediately took vengeance on me by downloading my entire credit history into the conference. He had hacked into the core of TRW, an institution that had made my business their business, extracting from it an abbreviated and incorrect version of my personal financial life. With this came the implication that he and Acid could and would then revise it to my disadvantage if I didn't back off.

Now, I had been in redneck bars with shoulder-length curls, in police custody while tripping on acid, and in Harlem long after midnight, but no one had ever put the spook in me quite the way Phiber Optik did at that moment. I was dealing with someone who had both the means and desire to leave me trapped in a life of wrinkled bills and money order queues. Never again would I be able to call The Sharper Image on a whim.

If someone was about to paralyze me with a digital spell, I wanted a more visceral sense of who he really was than could ever fit through a modem. So I wrote Optik a personal email in which I said, "We have obviously exceeded the bandwidth of this medium. Please give me a call and I won't insult your intelligence by giving you my number." It was listed, but I figured he wouldn't think that and would hack it out of the system and be on the phone with me right away. Which, of course, was exactly what happened.

In that conversation, as well as all the others that followed, I encountered an intelligent, civilized, and surprisingly principled eighteen-year-old kid who sounded as though he meant little harm to either man or data. Phiber Optik's hacking impulses seemed purely exploratory. I began to wonder if we wouldn't also have regarded spelunkers as desperate criminals if AT&T owned all the caves.

The terrifying poses that Phiber Optik and Acid Phreak had been striking on screen were actually just a media-amplified example of a universal form of human adaptation I had seen before: One becomes as he is beheld. They were both simply living up to what they thought we, and more particularly the editors of *Harper's Magazine,* expected of them.

As I became less their adversary and more their scoutmaster, I began getting "conference calls" in which six or eight members of the so-called Legion of Doom—by then an already legendary group of hackers—would crack pay phones all over New York and simultaneously land on my line in Wyoming. Most of them were so young that their voices hadn't yet changed. And I said, "Oh, I get it. You guys are *kids!* I see how it is. You want to violate the forbidden."

Months later, the editors of *Harper's* took Phiber Optik, Acid Phreak, and me to dinner at a fancy Chinese restaurant in Manhattan. Acid and Optik were both well scrubbed and fashionably clad. They looked to be about as dangerous as ducks. But as *Harper's* and the rest of the media had discovered to their great delight, the boys had developed distinctly showier personae for their rambles through the howling wilderness of what was not yet known as cyberspace.

There was no question that they were still making unauthorized use of data channels. On the night I finally met them in person for the first time, they left our restaurant table and disappeared into a phone booth for a long time. I didn't see them marshal any quarters to pay for the call before they left.

Around this time I also ingratiated myself with Emmanuel Goldstein, who was the guy behind *2600,* the semi-legal magazine of the hackers. His real name was Eric Corley; he took the name Emmanuel Goldstein from George Orwell's *1984.* You could not have chosen a better face to go with a guy who had a bomb in his hand. He *was* the guy with the bomb in his hand. Once he realized I was a friendly advocate in what you might call the straight world, he started feeding me stories about what had happened to Craig Neidorf and Steve Jackson.

In December 1988, a twenty-one-year-old Legion of Doomster in Atlanta named the Prophet had cracked a BellSouth computer and downloaded a three-page text file that outlined the marketing, servicing, upgrading, and billing administrative procedures and responsibilities for BellSouth's 911 system.

At some risk, I obtained a copy of this document. To read the whole thing straight through without immediately going into a coma would have required either a machine or a human being who'd had far too much practice thinking like one. Quite simply, it was the worst writing I had ever encountered in my entire life.

Since the document contained little that would have been of interest to anyone who was not a student of advanced organizational sclerosis, I assumed that the Prophet had copied the file only as a kind of hunting trophy. Having gone to the heart of the forest, he had returned with this coonskin to nail to the barn door.

The Prophet was so proud of his accomplishment that he copied the file onto a UNIX bulletin board in Lockport, Illinois. From there, it was downloaded by Craig Neidorf, also known as Knight Lightning, a pre-law student and one of the founding editors of *Phrack* magazine, an online publication that pretty much defined the hacker mentality of that time. When he got hold of the BellSouth document, he thought it would amuse his readers and reproduced it in the next issue of *Phrack*. He had little reason to think that he was doing something illegal because there was nothing in it to indicate that it contained proprietary or even sensitive information. Indeed, it closely resembled other Bell-South reference documents that had long been publicly available.

Rich Andrews, the systems operator who oversaw the operation of that UNIX bulletin board, thought there might be something funny about the document when he first ran across it in his system. To be on the safe side, he forwarded a copy of it to AT&T officials. He was then contacted by the authorities, with whom he fully cooperated, an act he would come to later regret.

On the basis of the foregoing events, a grand jury in Lockport was persuaded by the Secret Service in early February to hand down a seven-count indictment against the Prophet and Knight Lightning, charging them, among other things, with interstate transfer of stolen property worth more than $5,000. When the Prophet and two of his Georgia colleagues were arrested on February 7, 1990, the Atlanta newspapers reported they faced forty years in prison and a $2 million fine. Knight Lightning was arrested eight days later.

According to the indictment and BellSouth, the document was worth precisely $79,449. This astonishing figure turned out to be the value of the workstation on which the document had been typed. Far more detailed information could be ordered from BellSouth for thirteen bucks. Nonetheless, Craig faced a draconian jail sentence and a fine of $122,000. The authorities also seized his publication, *Phrack*, along with all related equipment, software, and data, including his list of subscribers, many of whom would soon lose their computers and data for the crime of having just appeared on this list.

When Emmanuel Goldstein told me about this, I said, "If they could shut down *Phrack*, couldn't they as easily shut down *2600*?" And he said, "I've got one advantage. I come out on paper and the Constitution knows how to deal with paper."

On January 24, 1990, a platoon of Secret Service agents entered the apartment Acid Phreak shared with his mother and twelve-year-old sister. The sister was the only person home when they burst through the door with guns drawn, but they somehow managed to hold her at bay for about half an hour until their quarry arrived.

By then, they were nearly done packing up all of Acid's worldly goods, including his computer, his notes, his books, and such dubiously dangerous tools as a telephone answering machine, a clock radio, and his complete collection of audiotapes.

One agent actually asked him to define the real purpose of the answering machine and was frankly skeptical when told that it answered the phone. Although the audiotapes seemed to contain nothing but music, who knew what kind of dark data Acid might have encoded between the notes of some James Hetfield solo on one of his Metallica albums?

When Acid Phreak's mother returned from work, she asked the agents exactly what her son had done to deserve all this attention and was told that, among other things, he had caused the AT&T system to crash several days earlier. The agent then explained that her darling boy was thought to have caused more than $1 billion in damage to the U.S. economy.

This accusation was never turned into a formal charge. Although the Secret Service maintained resolute possession of all of Acid Phreak's hardware, software, and data, no charge of any kind was ever filed against him. Across town, similar scenes were being played out at the homes of Phiber Optik and a Legion of Doom member named Scorpion. Again, equipment, notes, disks both hard and soft, and personal effects were confiscated. Again, no charges were ever filed.

On March 1, 1990, the Secret Service showed up at the offices of Steve Jackson Games, a company in Austin, Texas, that created and marketed all sorts of role-playing games. The agents ransacked the premises, broke into several locked filing cabinets, and eventually left carrying three computers, two laser printers, several hard disks, and several boxes of paper and floppy disks.

What had Steve Jackson Games done to deserve this nightmare? Although their role-playing games, of which Dungeons and Dragons was the most well known, had been accused of creating obsessive involvement in their nerdy young players, no one had ever before found it necessary to prevent their publication. The problem was that Steve Jackson had hired the wrong writer.

It turned out that the managing editor of Steve Jackson Games was a former hacker who was known to his fellow members in the Legion of Doom as the Mentor. At the time of the raid, he and the rest of the Jackson staff had been working for more than a year on a game called *GURPS Cyberpunk: High-Tech Low-Life Role-Playing.* The game resided entirely on the hard disks that the agents confiscated; indeed, this was their target. They told Jackson that, based on its author's background, they had reason to believe it was a "handbook for computer crime." It was therefore inappropriate for publication, First Amendment or no First Amendment.

I obtained a copy of the game from the trunk of the Mentor's car in an Austin parking lot. Like the BellSouth document, it seemed pretty innocuous to me, if a little inscrutable. Borrowing its flavor from the works of William Gibson and Austin sci-fi author Bruce Sterling, it was filled with silicon brain implants, holodecks, and Gauss guns. The cover copy described it as "a fusion of the dystopian visions of George Orwell and Timothy Leary." Actually, it portrayed a future like what Steve Jackson Games was just now experiencing at the hands of the Secret Service.

Over the course of the next three months, Steve Jackson estimated that his company lost about $125,000 in revenue because they had been unable to do business. Faced with that kind of fiscal hemorrhage, he couldn't afford to hire a lawyer to go after the Secret Service, who were no longer even returning his calls.

By then, he had asked both the state and national offices of the American Civil Liberties Union for help, and both had told him to run along. He also tried to go to the press. As in most other cases, they were unwilling to raise the alarm. As Jackson said at the time, "The conservative press is taking the attitude that the suppression of evil hackers is a good thing and that anyone who happens to be put out of business in the meantime . . . well, that's just their tough luck."

After a good deal of negotiation, Jackson was finally able to get the Secret Service to let him have some of his data back. But they told him he would be limited to an hour and a half on only one of his three computers to copy his data. Also, according to Jackson, "They insisted that all the copies be made by a Secret Service agent who was a two-finger typist. So we didn't get much."

In the end, Jackson and his staff had to reconstruct most of the game from neural rather than magnetic memory. Fortunately, they had a few old backups and had retrieved some scraps that had been passed around to game testers. They also had the determination of the enraged.

Taken together, these raids marked the beginning of the visible phase of Operation Sun Devil, a two-year Secret Service investigation that involved 150 federal agents, numerous local and state law enforcement agencies, and the combined security resources of PacBell, AT&T, Bellcore, BellSouth, MCI, U.S. Sprint, Southwestern Bell, NYNEX, U.S. West, and American Express.

The focus of this impressive institutional array was none other than the Legion of Doom, which then numbered less than twenty hackers, nearly all of them in their teens or early twenties. When I asked Acid Phreak why they had chosen such a threatening name for themselves, he said, "We didn't want to call ourselves something like the Legion of Flower Pickers. But the media ate it right up, probing the Legion of Doom like it was a gang or something, when really it was just a bunch of geeks behind computer terminals."

On May 8, 1990, Operation Sun Devil swept over the Legion of Doom and its ilk like a bureaucratic tsunami. The U.S. Secret Service served twenty-seven search warrants in fourteen cities ranging from Plano, Texas, to New York. In what they no doubt thought was an incredibly clever stroke of the imagination, they had named the operation after the football stadium at Arizona State University in Phoenix, which was not far from the Secret Service headquarters where all the raids had been planned.

In a press release issued the day after the nationwide sweep, the Secret Service boasted that they had shut down numerous computer bulletin boards, confiscated forty computers, and seized 23,000 disks. They also noted that "the conceivable criminal violations of this operation have serious implications for the health and welfare of all individuals, corporations, and United States Government agencies relying on computers and telephones to communicate."

It was unclear from their statement whether "this operation" referred to the Legion of Doom or Operation Sun Devil. But there was definitely room to interpret it either way. Aside from the three-page BellSouth document, the hackers had neither removed nor damaged anyone's data. Operation Sun Devil, on the other hand, had "serious implications" for a number of folks who relied on "computers and telephones to communicate."

All told, the people who were raided that day lost the equivalent of about 5.4 million pages of information—not to mention more than a few computers and telephones. Once Operation Sun Devil was over, transit through the wide-open spaces of the virtual world was a lot trickier than it had ever been before. The law had come to what was still not yet known as cyberspace.

The welfare of many of those associated with these people was also put in jeopardy. Like the single mother and computer consultant in Baltimore whose sole means of supporting herself and her eighteen-year-old son was taken away early one morning after Secret Service agents broke down her door with sledge hammers, entered with guns drawn, and seized all her computer equipment. Apparently, this was because her son had also been using it.

Or the father in New York City who opened his door at six A.M. one day only to find a shotgun pointed at his nose. A dozen agents entered, and while one of them kept the man's wife in a choke hold, the rest made ready to shoot as they entered the bedroom of their sleeping fourteen-year-old child. Before leaving, the agents confiscated every piece of electronic equipment in the house, including all the telephones.

Not surprisingly, no one in the newspaper business seemed particularly worried about any of this. Along with the rest of the "straight" media, they were too obsessed by what they portrayed as disruptions of emergency services as well as the awful sociopathic actions of all those involved in such activities. One report expressed relief that no one appeared to have died as a result of all these "intrusions" that had been carried out by the hackers.

Finally, the Secret Service rewarded the good citizenship of Rich Andrews by confiscating his computer along with all the email, both read and unread, that his subscribers had left on it. Like many others whose equipment and data had been taken by the Secret Service, Andrews was not charged with anything. But they inflicted on him the worst punishment that any computer nerd could suffer: data death. Or, as Andrews said at the time, "I'm the one that found it. I'm the one that turned it in. And I'm the one that is suffering."

Insofar as the Secret Service was concerned, association with stolen data was all the guilt they needed to come for you. It was as if the government could seize your house simply because some guest had left a stolen VCR in an upstairs bedroom closet. The first concept of modern jurisprudence to have arrived in what was still not yet known as cyberspace was zero tolerance.

As I kept on hearing more and more about the vile injustices that had been heaped on my young pals in the Legion of Doom—not to mention also the unfortunate folks who happened to be nearby—I drifted back into a sixties-style sense of the government as a thing of monolithic evil efficiency. I also quickly developed an up-against-the-wall willingness to spit out words such as *pig* or *fascist* about what they had done.

Although these events have now pretty much been forgotten in a digital world where people would like to believe nothing like it could ever happen again, they led to a visit from the FBI that entirely changed my life.

THIRTY-ONE

A VISIT FROM THE FBI

While sitting in my office in Pinedale one day in May 1990, I got a phone call. A voice said, "Hi, this is Special Agent Richard Baxter, Jr." Wyoming is a small town with very long streets, and I had already met Agent Baxter when he had come up from Rock Springs to do an FBI background check on John Turner before he became the director of the U.S. Fish and Wildlife Service. Agent Baxter had also helped me out with some livestock theft.

He had always been kind of laconic, but now he seemed anxious and I'd never known him to be like that. I said, "What is this about?" And he said, "I can't discuss it on the phone. Can we talk in person?" Now I was thinking, *Oh God, that's not good.* Everyone knew I was associated with one of the most notorious bands in the world as far as drugs were concerned. Could it be they had finally decided to come get the Grateful Dead and were going to pick us all off one by one?

When he arrived, Agent Baxter was definitely squirming. It turned out that he was hoping to discover if by any chance I had been the angry hacker who, in May 1989, had gotten hold of a chunk of the highly secret source code that drove the Apple Macintosh computer and distributed it to a variety of addresses, while claiming responsibility in the name of the Nu Prometheus League, a group of anonymous hackers, some of whom had been Apple employees.

Not surprisingly, Apple was totally freaked out. All they really had to offer the world was the software that had been encoded on the ROM chip of every Macintosh. This set of instructions was the cyber DNA that made a Macintosh a Macintosh. Even worse was the fact that a good deal of the magic in this code had been put there by people who no longer worked for Apple and would do so again only if they were encouraged with cattle prods. Apple's attitude toward its ROM code was a little like that of a rich kid toward his inheritance: Not actually knowing how to create wealth himself, he guards what he has with hysterical fervor.

Because poor Agent Baxter didn't know a ROM chip from a Vise-Grip, I had to spend a lot of time trying to educate him about the nature of precisely what it was that had been stolen. For a good couple of hours, I did my best to explain that the crime he was investigating may not have been actually committed before giving him a pretty solid defense as to why, if indeed it had, I had not committed it.

Even after I had done this, I wouldn't swear that Agent Baxter ever quite got his mind around it. When I showed him some actual source code, gave him a demonstration of email in action, and downloaded a file from the WELL, he took to rubbing his face with both hands while peering at me over his fingertips and saying things like, "Whooo-ee! It sure is something, isn't it? My eight-year-old knows more about these things than I do." He made this last remark not so much with a father's pride as an immigrant's fear of a strange new land into which he had been forcibly moved. When Agent Baxter looked across my keyboard into cyberspace, he most definitely did not like what he saw.

Why had Agent Baxter come all the way to Pinedale to investigate a crime he didn't understand that had occurred in five different places, none of which was within five hundred miles of my office? Because Apple had told the FBI that owing to the virulent sentiment against them in and around the Silicon Valley, they could expect little or no cooperation from hackers there. They had advised the FBI to question only hackers who were as far away as possible from the twisted heart of the subculture. Although I was not a hacker, this group somehow included me.

Agent Baxter didn't know source code from Tuesday, but he did know that Apple Computer had told his agency that what had been stolen from them and then widely disseminated was the complete recipe for a Macintosh computer. The distribution of this secret formula might result in the creation of millions of Macintoshes not made by Apple, and ultimately the eventual ruination of the company.

In fact, what had actually been distributed was just a small portion of the code that related specifically to Color QuickDraw, Apple's name for the software that controlled the Mac's on-screen graphics. But this was yet another detail that Agent Baxter could not comprehend. For all he knew, you could grow Macintoshes from floppy disks.

I explained to him that Apple was alleging something like the ability to assemble an entire human being from the recipe for a foot, but even he knew that this analogy was inexact. Trying to get him to accept the idea that a corporation could go mad with suspicion was quite futile because he had a far different perception of the emotional reliability of institutions.

Eventually, I learned the real reason Agent Baxter had come to see me was because the FBI thought that whoever had done this had also probably gone to that hackers' conference I had attended in San Francisco. They had been doing surveillance on it. And so while Agent Baxter was not quite coming to arrest me, he was collecting evidence.

During the course of our extended conversation that day, Agent Baxter asked me about Mitch Kapor, who had written Lotus 1-2-3. By then, I had already done an interview with Mitch for *MicroTimes* magazine in Silicon Valley. We were friends, and a less likely computer terrorist would have been hard to come by. As it turned out, Mitch was one of the few corporate people who had also been visited by the bureau. That the FBI would want to question him about anything made Mitch very upset.

That night, I posted a ten-thousand-word essay entitled "Crime and

Puzzlement" on the WELL in which I discussed all these matters in great detail. "In over-reaching as extravagantly as they did," I wrote, "the Secret Service may actually have done a service for those of us who love liberty. They have provided us with a devil. And devils, among their other galvanizing virtues, are just great for clarifying the issues and putting iron in your spine. In the presence of a devil, it's always easier to figure out where you stand."

As I was writing "Crime and Puzzlement," I was diddling around looking for something to call this brave new virtual world in which we were all just beginning to live. I had read *Neuromancer* by William Gibson and in it, a voice-over says,

> Cyberspace. A consensual hallucination experienced daily by billions of legitimate operators, in every nation, by children being taught mathematical concepts . . . A graphic representation of data abstracted from the banks of every computer in the human system. Unthinkable complexity. Lines of light ranged in the nonspace of the mind, clusters and constellations of data. Like city lights, receding.

Although Gibson was the one who had coined the word, which he spelled with a capital *C*, and was then given due credit for having done so in the Oxford English Dictionary, I decided to begin employing the term in what has become its present usage. The way I defined it back then, cyberspace is where you are when you are on the phone. Cyberspace is where your money is.

In my essay, I wrote,

> Cyberspace, in its present condition, has a lot in common with the 19th Century West. It is vast, unmapped, culturally and legally ambiguous, verbally terse (unless you happen to be a court stenographer), hard to get around in, and up for grabs. Large institutions already claim to own the place, but most of the actual natives are solitary and independent, sometimes to the point of sociopathy. It

is, of course, a perfect breeding ground for both outlaws and new ideas about liberty.

Several days after I had posted "Crime and Puzzlement," Mitch Kapor, who was also a denizen of the WELL, happened to read it on his laptop while flying from Boston to San Francisco in his Canadair bizjet. Suddenly, he felt like there was somebody he could talk to about all this. A man who placed great emphasis on face-to-face contact, Mitch called me up from his plane somewhere over Nebraska and asked if he could land in Pinedale.

After Mitch had literally dropped in on me from out of the sky, I started filling him in on everything I knew. All the while, he grew increasingly anxious. As a spring snowstorm swirled outside my office, we talked for a couple of hours, and Mitch decided the time had come for him to speak up about all this as well.

Both of us felt like we had been burned in various ways by organizations in the past, and so we were anti-organization. But we also thought we could bloody the government's nose in a few of the Sun Devil cases and get them to understand that the First Amendment applied to cyberspace as well as the physical world. Which was how the Electronic Frontier Foundation came about.

THIRTY-TWO

EFF

I had imagined that Mitch and I would be doing kind of a *Butch Cassidy and the Sundance Kid* thing, but it became apparent almost immediately that it was going to require more than two fierce guys to get the job done, even if one of them had a ferocity backed by great wealth. We began it all by announcing that we were going to legally constitute the Electronic Frontier Foundation as a two- or possibly three-man organization that would raise and disburse funds for education, lobbying, and litigation in areas relating to digital speech as well as the extension of the protections guaranteed by the Constitution into cyberspace.

On the strength of preliminary stories about our efforts that had run in the *Washington Post* and the *New York Times,* Mitch received an offer from Steve Wozniak to match whatever funds he was going to dedicate to this effort. Although Woz wanted to be in right away, it was another thing entirely to actually get his money. And so before that ever happened, I got an email from John Gilmore saying, "I don't have resources like Mitch or Wozniak, but I can do a hundred grand.

Would that help?" And I said, "Yes." Pretty quickly, we had more than a quarter of a million dollars to get the Electronic Frontier Foundation started.

Our intent was to have the EFF fund, conduct, and support legal efforts to demonstrate that during Operation Sun Devil, the Secret Service had exercised prior restraint on publications, limited free speech, carried out improper seizures of equipment and data, used undue force, and generally conducted itself in a fashion that was arbitrary, oppressive, and unconstitutional.

Although we knew that acting on behalf of hackers, who were generally beyond public sympathy, was not going to be popular no matter who else might benefit from the results in the long run, our goal was to ensure that all electronic speech would be protected just as certainly as any opinions that were printed or, for that matter, screamed. We wanted to clarify issues surrounding the distribution of intellectual property and help create for America a future as blessed by the Bill of Rights as its past had always been.

Mitch and I decided that the situation merited the services of a kick-ass free-speech advocacy law firm such as Rabinowitz, Boudin, who had defended Daniel Ellsberg on charges that he had stolen the Pentagon Papers. Leonard Boudin's daughter, Kathy, was a member of the Weather Underground and had survived the explosion that destroyed a Greenwich Village town house and killed three other Weathermen in 1970. Michael Standard, another partner at the firm, had been representing Timothy Leary when he escaped from prison and gone into exile in Algeria. So I figured I was definitely talking to the right firm to represent us in this undertaking.

Mitch and I hadn't yet talked about money, but any time you specifically don't talk about money, you are talking about money. And so when Mitch asked me to tell a lawyer named Harvey Silverglate everything I knew about Operation Sun Devil, the inference was that Mitch would help support the costs that are always liable to arise whenever you tell a lawyer anything. In the conference call that followed with more of the associates at the firm, I could almost hear the skeletal click as all the lawyers' jaws dropped. The next day, two representatives from the firm met with Acid Phreak, Phiber Optik, and Scorpion.

On July 10, 1990, Mitch and I formally announced the establishment of the EFF at a press conference in Washington, D.C. We met with a slew of congressional staffers, legal authorities, and journalists, as well as officials from the White House and the Library of Congress, thereby beginning discussions that we expected would continue over a period of years. We also applied for and were granted 501(c)(3) status, which meant that all contributions to the EFF would be tax deductible.

As we were gearing up, an interesting bit of ironic serendipity occurred. At one point after I had become infuriated with Operation Sun Devil, I had called the American Civil Liberties Union. Basically they told me to go fuck myself. But they also put me in touch with Jerry Berman, one of the great Washington, D.C. log rollers who had been their chief legislative counsel as well as the founder and director of ACLU Projects on Privacy and Information Technology.

I called Jerry and told him why I was so concerned about Operation Sun Devil, and he just brushed me off, saying, "Oh, you don't need me to do that." But after what we were working on had filtered around his office, Jerry got on it. He then began to unleash the considerable resources of John Podesta, the former chief minority counsel for the Senate Judiciary Subcommittee on Patents, Copyrights, and Trademarks, who had just cofounded a powerful lobbying firm then known as Podesta Associates. Podesta would later go on to become Bill Clinton's chief of staff (and eventually face a notorious hacking problem of his own during Hillary Clinton's 2016 presidential campaign), but even then he was one very powerful guy to have on our side.

By then, Mitch had started a new company that he was fully expecting to go big because its intended purpose was to make it possible for people to do lightning-fast searches of their hard drive for any text string. To this day, I'm baffled as to why it never became a huge deal. He had gotten himself a bunch of office space in Cambridge, Massachusetts, so right away we had a place for our staff to work. Basically, we had somebody there to answer the phone, one lawyer in-house, and one lawyer on retainer from Rabinowitz, Boudin.

Mitch and I had become the Laurel and Hardy of cyberspace. We began filing suits and winning them. We hadn't been at it very long at all before we both realized that this was going to go on for all of our natural lives—it was going to go on for centuries into the future. And that future society, if it managed to exist at all, was going to have to work hard to assimilate all of these changes.

At a certain point, Mitch decided that, for financial reasons and because it was too far outside the halls of power, he wanted to shut down the Cambridge office. So we moved to a big office on M Street in D.C., where we started to behave like a Washington special interest group. We were lobbying and producing court positions and lobbying and suing and lobbying and suing. That was all Jerry Berman's doing because by then he had become our executive director.

Although John Gilmore was not really a founder of the EFF, he was definitely a sustainer. At one point, it was just him and me, and we left Washington, D.C., and brought the EFF to San Francisco, where it was located for a while in Toad Hall, the house that John owns in the Panhandle in which I now live.

John and I have both derived something from our uneasy relationship because in many ways, it is exactly like my uneasy relationship with Weir. With Weir, I always want something much more ordered, like a comfortable rhyming scheme in a song while he insists on inserting all these additional syllables into my lyrics. In terms of my work with John on the EFF, *he* has always been the guy who said, "No, there can only be five syllables in that." In other words, he is like me in our relationship.

Insofar as Mitch, John, and myself are concerned, this funny kind of serendipity came into play where three clouds that were rotating around one another came into synchrony and ended up producing the Electronic Frontier Foundation, as well as a bunch of other stuff that then became my mission for the next twenty-three years of my life.

Aside from Operation Sun Devil, a lot of things that had come before helped draw me into doing this. Writing songs for the Grateful Dead taught me that a jealous view of copyright was not necessarily in one's own best interest. If you were particular about copies being made of your material—something that at that time was still considered to be theft—this did not work to your advantage. The Dead would let anyone tape their shows but not sell those tapes, which led to the creation of a real community.

In a lot of ways, the band prefigured Internet culture. When I first went looking for Deadheads on Usenet, it turned out that this was a good place to find them because it was the only available agora that could then be had. It was a pure connection, and so I was slotted in. By virtue of having been associated so closely with the Dead, I obtained a lot of unearned authority, but that was okay with me. I was willing to take what I could get because I had already been dealing with power politics for a long while, and any time you can get something for free in politics, you take it.

Suddenly, I felt unbounded. Unlike all of the time I had spent as an environmentalist in Wyoming, I now had a constituency that was not defined by previously formed political views. The initial settings had not yet been applied, so I could help apply them. I had already developed a sufficiently credible voice so that people would pay attention to what I wanted to say. Self-publishing opened me up as a writer, and what I was writing about was the developing economics, politics, and law of cyberspace. Oddly enough, no one else seemed to be.

Not that there weren't sometimes serious repercussions to the views I was now expressing on the Internet on a fairly regular basis. Inspired by an astonishing quote from Thomas Jefferson as well as my own experience with the Grateful Dead's willingness to give away our music to people who had taped our concerts, I published an essay in *Wired* magazine in 1994 that was variously called "The Economy of Ideas," "Wine Without Bottles," and "Everything You Know About Intellectual Property Is Wrong."

I realized that with the Internet, it would be possible for anybody to make infinite copies of any work that could be created by the human mind and then distribute them at zero cost throughout the entire portion of humanity that was interested. This was going to change everything.

Although I thought that most of these ideas were so obvious as to be noncontroversial, I soon learned how wrong I was. In fact, they were anathema to companies like Microsoft, who made their living by bottling thought. As soon as "The Economy of Ideas" appeared in *Wired*, Bill Gates, who had been one of most substantial supporters of the Electronic Frontier Foundation, withdrew both his own and his company's support. Moreover, he let it be known that any major contribution to EFF from a Microsoft employee could be grounds for dismissal. This despite the fact that I had not written the essay ex cathedra as the EFF, but as a statement of my own opinion.

And so it was that the other great work of my life began: spending countless hours and air miles tramping around the planet trying to convince the powers-that-have-been of the complete futility of their methods for making money from thought. Despite the many travails I encountered along the way, I would rank cofounding the Electronic Frontier Foundation as one of the major achievements of my life. After having served as its vice-chairman for twenty-seven years, my formal position with the organization is now listed as "Rocking Chair."

THIRTY-THREE

TIMOTHY LEARY REDUX

A s I fell deeper down the rabbit hole of digital technology, I gravi-
tated toward virtual reality, which in many ways was pretty much
what I had been into all along. In 1987, I saw a picture of the data
glove on the cover of *Scientific American* and a bell went off. I knew immediately that something was going on and that maybe it was time to
revisit my notion of how one interacted with these rough beasts called
computers. If one could actually reach into the data sphere and grab
hold of it with a hand, that was completely different from doing so on
a keyboard.

In any event, I became enchanted with people who were involved in
this new form of technology, and I met a fellow named Erik Gullikson,
who was working on a virtual reality project at Autodesk. He thought it
might be a good idea to recruit Timothy Leary to include virtual reality
as part of his latest medicine show.

By then, Tim had been in prison and in exile in Algeria and had
then spent more time in prison only to emerge and somehow become
the toast of the town in Los Angeles. He was living in a house in

Beverly Hills with Barbara, his fifth wife, going out to clubs on the Sunset Strip about every night, delivering three or four lectures a week at colleges and universities for ten or twelve thousand dollars a pop, and playing small parts in movies and television shows.

Although I had not seen Tim since I had spent time with him and the Grateful Dead at Millbrook in 1967, I went down to Los Angeles to interview him for the book I was still purportedly writing. At this point, I had been off mind-altering substances for a long time. The first person I met in the house was Barbara, who said that before I could even talk to Tim I had to eat some of these brownies. Which of course I did.

The three of us then went out on this wild cruise through the hills where we got totally lost. Barbara was screeching at us like a harpy, and Tim and I were laughing like crazy and bucking her authority. It was like he had found an ally in me. The two of us were catching up on old times and new times. It was a truly wonderful night as well as the birth of a brand-new deal between us.

The way I understood the deal was that periodically, we would have these intense distilled encapsulated familial Irish moments. Blood was not even thick enough to describe the nature of our new relationship, because we were both outlaws in the primordial sense of the term. As Bob Dylan had once famously said, to live outside the law you had to be honest on a certain level. You can't be a proper outlaw without some kind of touchstone of deep morality, and Tim and I understood that about each other. Just like him, I also loved state change. How about we try this and see what happens? Life endangering? Too bad.

This was truly a Nietzschean condition that was beyond good and evil. It was recognizing that you had a message to share that was far beyond this binary framework, and if they judged you, then they judged you. You had to absorb that, but it had little to do with your real purpose in life.

If I looked at Tim's purpose in life and mine, it was all about trying to demonstrate to humanity that reality was an opinion and not a fact. And that authority was not God-given but earned and also transitory.

Once we began spending time together again, Tim introduced me to people as the most American person he knew. It was intended to be both a compliment and an insult. "Here's Barlow. He's an American."

Although I had always been proud of my ability to not judge people, Timmy pressed harder on that than anybody I had ever known. He wanted to force you into this point of choice where if you were going to judge him, you had both ample opportunity and plenty of evidence. He gave us all so much rope to hang him with that in the final analysis, not many people who really knew him were actually willing to use it. Those who didn't know him judged him harshly, and they had every reason to do so because of how much damage he had done by espousing the use of LSD as the sole solution to all of the world's many problems.

Tim was all about real redemption, and while it is easy to redeem the holy, it is far more important to redeem the base and the depraved. It's easy to love your friends, but what Christ asked us to do was love our enemies. It's easy to forgive the minor transgressions but not the real sins, and that's where it all really comes down.

Tim's morality, such as it existed at all, was incredibly flexible. If you looked at yourself as a freewheeling instrument of the God-knows-what—which I think he did and I certainly did as well—you never knew when you were actually being summoned to do something important as an agent of instruction and when you were just acting out.

Tim knew he was catalytic and that real catalytic behavior has no moral reference. You just smelled the air and made your decision on the basis of things that did not have rules. Throughout his life, Tim went back and forth between being a good Irish boy and the devil's top hand.

Tim viewed love as both a necessity and a weakness. He was really the most complex, divided human being I had ever met. The Catholic Church was always the deal for Tim. It was the heart of the matter, and he spent most of his life being the anti-Christ while at the same time wanting to be the Christ.

Tim also worshipped at the altar of all that was female. When I reconnected with him in Los Angeles, he and Barbara had been married for about twelve years. I always saw her as something the devil wore when he was in a particularly sporting mood. She was dire and difficult but also a wonderful human being in an extremely weird way. She was the great love of his life. Tim said that to me numerous times.

I began spending a good deal of time with them, and then Tim basically gave me permission to be her lover. He couldn't be for her what she needed sexually, so it made more sense for him to anoint someone to do that for him. We had a wild relationship.

At one point, Tim and I went off on a speaking tour together in Europe. It was right after his daughter, Susan, had committed suicide by hanging herself from the bars of her jail cell after she had twice been found mentally unfit to stand trial for having shot her boyfriend in the head while he was sleeping. In many ways, Tim was still possessed by this and very much of an emotional mess.

I was much more of a moralist than Tim, and thought the best way to judge a person was by their children. Thus, I felt that the man who in some weird way was now my master had failed the ultimate test. While we were in Europe, I was out on the road acting as his foil with this terrible sense of "You are the ultimate loser, pal." I tried to get him to talk to me about it, but he could never explain why his daughter had died this way. He spoke about her suicide with the terrible abstraction of pain while alternately blaming himself. He did not have a position about it; actually, he had so many that they added up to not being one. He was really deeply troubled by her death and never did manage to work it out.

Part of Tim's thing about boredom was that in boredom lies responsibility. In that still moment when nothing else is going on, you actually have to confront yourself. And that was the last thing he ever wanted to do. The bargain Tim had made with himself was that he was denied a view of his own soul until the very last moments of his life.

But he really was a messenger. Only someone so demonic and so equivocal about all the normal tendencies of morality and faith and decency could have been the proper vessel for the spiritual message that Timothy Leary brought to the world. He was possessed. He was a demon. A very special demon. In order to spread the message, one of the fallen had to rise up. And that was Timothy Leary.

I honestly believe Timothy Leary was the handmaiden of God in the strangest possible way. I'd always felt that one of the people in Christianity who got the short shrift was Judas. Without Judas, what would there have been? No crucifixion, no resurrection, and no redemption. You had to have Judas. Somebody had to be the Judas, and that was absolutely who Tim was. I knew he would never betray me, because in many ways, I was as bad as he was.

THIRTY-FOUR

WHO'S NeXT

I met Steve Jobs for the first time because I wanted to go to the introduction of the NeXT computer at Davies Symphony Hall in San Francisco on October 12, 1988. I contacted some people I knew at NeXT and then I got a letter from Steve asking if I was the same John Barlow who had written songs for the Grateful Dead. I told him I was and he said, "And you want to write about the NeXT?" After I told him I did, Steve said he would get me a press pass.

At that point, Steve was scared shitless and for good reason. Apple had tossed him out on his ear, and with NeXT he was completely on his own. In many ways, he was actually totally on his ass but also being realistic. When I looked at that machine, I turned to him and said, "Jeez, this is the greatest technological tool ever devised. This completely blows all the competition out of the water. You're going to do so well." And he said, "In my experience, more companies have died of indigestion than starvation." By *indigestion* he meant having more demand than he could fulfill, which of course was not a problem he had or was ever going to have with the NeXT.

In the end, Steve managed to sell only forty-two thousand of those things. Primarily, this was because they were too far ahead of their time and much too expensive. The company was also too slow in coming up with alternatives to the things that were wrong with it. Steve was convinced—and I don't know where he got this idea—that the answer to storage in the future would be these big 650-megabyte read-write optical disks. You could plug them in and out and that was your world. It was the operating system and also held all of your documents. The company went on trying to get people to use those optical disks as the main means of storage a lot longer than they should have.

But the machines were incredibly practical and so much faster than anything else at the time. They also had a whole bunch of features that have not been seen in computers since. The NeXT had something called display postscript, which meant that it wrote postscript to the screen and to the printer so that whatever was on the screen was exactly what you would have on the printer. It was all written in Objective-C, which was not a popular computer language then, but now all the apps in iPhones are written in it; the iPhone is actually a NeXT, as is the MacBook.

What Steve had brought with him from Apple to NeXT was the operating system. If you go into the iPhone now and poke around, you'll find a whole bunch of files that have the extension *nib*, which actually stands for NeXT Interface Builder. Back then, these files were an incredibly powerful leap forward.

I just loved that machine. Though, like Steve, it had some really astonishing flaws. Unlike Steve, the NeXT's flaws were corrected. They were corrected pretty quickly but not until after they had already put a mark against it.

In 1991, I became the associate editor of *NeXTWORLD*, a magazine devoted exclusively to the NeXT computer. *NeXTWORLD* was not a direct extension of NeXT itself, but if I wrote something that Steve didn't like, a seven A.M. phone call from him was something that could happen at least once a week. The magazine itself didn't have a huge amount of subscribers but you talk about fanboys? I was definitely one of them.

Even then, Steve himself was kind of impossible to characterize. You would have this immediate strong desire to both hug him and slug him. You didn't know which was stronger, but they were both pretty powerful. Steve was not like Dick Cheney or Bill Gates. They both had blazingly fast central processors, whereas Steve was also charismatic to the tits. Steve made you care about what he thought of you, and even though you could pretend that you didn't, you were kidding yourself. It was a quality Garcia had as well, but the thing with him was that he didn't want you to care about him like that. He really did not, but nevertheless you did.

On May 22, 1993, Steve asked me if I would host his celebrity roast at the NeXT convention at the Moscone Center in San Francisco. Roasts are usually meted out to people who are doing well, but the somewhat hollow quality of this roast might actually have been the nadir of Steve's career. The NeXT was already failing as a hardware play, which was really sad because it was far and away the greatest computer ever made. The elegance of design was like UNIX by Armani.

The NeXT had been introduced at a time when Steve firmly believed he was going to make it a success. But then there was this era of darkness when Steve decided that what he really had was a software company, and he hated that. One of Steve's main principles was that he wanted to integrate both software and hardware. Only by doing that could he control the entire user experience, which made really good sense.

My roast of him that night consisted mainly of gallows humor about the state of the company. I was aware of the pall hanging over the event, and I was trying to make light of it in a dark way. What I had completely forgotten about was that Steve had just married Laurene Powell, and so I now had a fierce contender for his interests. On the conference floor in the Moscone Center the next day, she came at me with both spike heels right down my throat and lathered me up and down. Like, "How dare you say that stuff? We thought you were a loyal partisan." I said, "I am a loyal partisan, but if NeXT is still manufacturing hardware next year at this time, I will eat the column I wrote in which I claimed that it wouldn't."

She said, "Steve is not going to be happy to hear you said that." I said, "I don't care whether he's happy or not." The fact was that I did care. I couldn't not care about what Steve thought. But Laurene in full dudgeon was nobody to mess with.

To his credit, Steve himself never came at me about it, because he wanted to have a good relationship with me. And he already knew the hardware wasn't going to work because the model was too expensive. He also really cared about the Dead. In our conversation before the roast, I realized what a fanboy Steve was, because he was talking about dropping acid and how important that and the music of the Grateful Dead had been for him.

One aspect of Steve's genius was his ability to surround himself with people like Bud Tribble, whom those at Apple used to call "the world's smartest invertebrate." Steve would fulminate and carry on and punch the wall and tell people what idiots they were and then flounce out of the room. And then Bud, who had been sitting there quietly all the while, would say, "Here's what he meant." He would pick up the pieces, like Jony Ive has done at Apple for the past twenty-five years.

At one point, the president of Volkswagen got in touch with me. He wanted me to introduce him to Steve because he had something important to talk to him about. I said, "What is it?" And he said, "Does that matter?" And I said, "Yes, it actually does because as important as this may seem to you, it may not be important to him."

I had to go through a whole rigmarole getting the two of them together. By then, Steve was back at Apple. What the guy wanted to do was produce an iCar, but this was in 2004, just as Steve was beginning to create the iPhone. Steve said, "You know, I love this idea. I really do. But I've got this other thing I'm doing, and I'm not going to do anything else until I've gotten it right." The Volkswagen guy was like, "But I'm going to be spending all the money on this." And Steve's thing was, "No, you don't get it. I'm changing the world." It probably set back the development of the self-driving car for a while.

On every level, Steve was a trip. He truly was, and I really miss him. After he started getting sick, I went to his office one day to talk to him about something. When some people are dying, it can be good for them to broach the subject and talk about it openly. But there was no way in hell Steve was going to do that. To his way of thinking, he was not dying. He was not. He had done some other challenging things in his life, and he was going to beat this as well.

I never think of people as being happy or satisfied. On a good day, Jerry Garcia was joyful and so was Steve. I saw him experience glee many times. He would give these demos introducing a product and somehow in spite of the fact that they were not ready to give the demo at all, it would work and he would be delighted. But there would be other times when it would work and he would *still* just be kicking himself all the way up the aisle.

In his fascist way, Steve imposed a lot of syntactic conventions that have made it a lot easier for users to interface with all the gnarly stuff that happens down close to the metal within their own devices. For Steve, that was a serious part of the proposition because he was a fanatic about design and didn't ever think of it as a decal that you put on top.

For Steve, design was something that went all the way to the core, and he knew there weren't many people who understood that. It's hard to say where that came from, but what I do know for certain is that we will never see his like again.

MEETING CYNTHIA

R ight across from the banquet room in which the Steve Jobs celebrity roast was about to take place, the American Psychiatric Association was having a session of its annual conference. I was standing outside the entrance before going in to roast Steve and all the psychiatrists were milling around in their corner and I saw this tall, slender woman with long blond hair in a very crisp Armani suit.

Even before I saw her face, I knew I was in love with her in a way I had thought was fictional. I had never experienced anything like it in my entire life. She was standing with her back to me, and then she turned and looked right at me over her left shoulder. Her gaze was direct and penetrating and went on for a long time.

I had always thought that the idea of love at first sight was a literary monster created to make people feel less satisfied about what they had, and I could not imagine any mechanism that would cause it to actually take place. But we locked in on this beam, and I felt like I was having a hallucination and hearing voices. The whole thing was so dreamlike that I stepped back and rubbed my eyes and tried to figure out what I was going to do about it. Before this woman and I had ever said any-thing to each other, I felt I had finally found my other half.

Whatever was going on between us, I was not going to let the mo-ment pass without investigation. So I circled her a couple of times. Once I realized she was not going into the Steve Jobs roast but into the psychiatrists' meeting, I hustled over and said, "Look, this is pre-sumptuous of me but you are something." And she said, "So are you." I said, "Where are you from?" And she said, "A little town in British Columbia." I said, "I'm from a little town in Wyoming, which is sort of similar. Where do you live now?" And she said, "New York." I said, "Me too."

I told her where I lived and she said, "Oh, that's very interesting." I said, "Why?" And she said, "I just rented an apartment in that building to be my office." In fact, she had rented the apartment precisely two floors above mine.

She had to go into her meeting, so I said, "If you get out of your thing before I get out of mine, please do me the favor of sticking around." We did not exchange names. I just told her to wait for me. Later that evening, I was busy running the roast when I looked up and saw her standing at the back of the room.

This hacker I knew who was a strange character was there that night and he said, "I can see what's happening to you, Barlow. But I've got some bad news for you. That woman has a diamond the size of the Rock of Gibraltar on her finger. She's married." I hadn't seen the ring yet, but when I did, I knew it hadn't come out of a Cracker Jack box. To that point, I had studiously avoided noticing it, but I said, "We'll see how married she really is."

I took her to the roast after-party and she immediately went off and flirted with every guy there but me. For some reason, I felt perfectly okay with that. It was just her way. Toward the end of the party, I came over to her and said, "Look, I would like to do something right now, but I know you're married and I hope it's okay with you." And she bent forward and let me kiss her. That was pretty much the ball game.

Her name was Cynthia Horner and she had grown up on Vancouver Island in Nanaimo, a beautiful old mill town right across the strait from Vancouver. One of the things that set it apart is that they have an annual bathtub race from Nanaimo to Vancouver. It's about thirty miles across the strait, and they sail it in bathtubs with outboard motors.

British Columbia is a part of the world that has a wonderfully well-developed sense of absurdist self-deprecating humor, and one of the things they love to make fun of is Nanaimo and its culture. Because Nanaimo is semi-isolated, the people there have come up with their own way of pronouncing quite a broad variety of words. They speak Nanaim-ese.

Both of Cynthia's parents were doctors. Her mother was a dermatologist and her father had grown up on a great big ranch south of Calgary. His side of the family included big-time politicians, like the Speaker of the Canadian Senate and the head of the Canadian National Railway. They were all right-wing ranchers in much the same way my father had been.

Cynthia had attended the public high school in Nanaimo and then gone to the University of British Columbia. After graduating from the medical school there, she had gone to the Mayo Clinic in Rochester, Minnesota, to become a psychiatrist.

The two of us spent the night together, but we did not make love. The next night, I was cohosting a party for a NeXT database software company whose only customer was the CIA. So everybody at the party was CIA. I knew these guys loved to feel hip, so I hired a theatrical group from San Francisco that was entirely composed of really enormous people who were crawling back and forth on heavy ropes over everyone at the party. You would look up and there would be three hundred pounds of flesh above you. It was art.

Cynthia had never taken a psychedelic before or ever done anything wild or bohemian in her life. She had never even smoked a joint, nothing. We took MDA together that night, and she loved MDA and she loved the party.

The next night, the Grateful Dead were playing at Cal Expo, the state fairgrounds in Sacramento, and we went backstage tripping on acid. Cynthia was not a music person at all, and the fact that I was a lyricist for the Dead was not particularly relevant to her. Even though she was the kind of person who would never have been caught dead at a Dead concert, Cynthia liked it a lot and thought the music was great and the Deadheads fascinating.

We were both so completely and hopelessly besotted with each other that I think I could have taken her to a dogfight and she would have thought it was okay. Even though she looked completely incongruous standing by the soundboard in her black Armani suit, Cynthia became a Deadhead.

We spent several more nights together without making love, and I found out a lot more about her marriage. While she had been at the Mayo Clinic, Cynthia had met Diego, who was from Argentina. On paper, he was a perfect match for her. Before anyone had even cracked any part of the eggshell on AIDS, he had been a rising star in research on the disease. I think his family was worth at least half a billion dollars.

Diego moved to New York to continue his AIDS research work, and Cynthia went with him to do her residency at Beth Israel hospital. They got married, once in secret and then again in a big splashy wedding in Nanaimo about six months before I met her. In every way, Diego was the answer to her parents' prayers.

When I met Cynthia, she and Diego had been together for a couple of years, but they were having problems. In some Latin cultures, a woman has two roles she can play. She can either be a Madonna or a whore. And nobody had ever explained that to Cynthia. After they got married, Diego wanted her to be a Madonna, and she was completely not into that. Cynthia was a pretty sexual being, and she'd already had a number of affairs before I met her.

As I found out more and more about her husband, I thought, "Jeez, I can't do this. I can't disrupt their marriage, and this guy is much better qualified to be married to her than I am. Truly." It was not self-effacing. It was just obvious to me. At one point, I said to her, "It's a good thing we haven't made love yet, because I think it's probably best for you to stay with your husband." And she said, "No, I think it's best that we do so you'll see why I am not going to."

We moved in together a week after we met. It was one of those completely unexpected acts of providence where two worlds collide and something wonderful comes from the point where they touch.

THIRTY-SIX

LIVING WITH HER

My time with Cynthia was the happiest I had ever been in my life. Many of those who saw us when we were together still talk about us, because it was an extraordinary thing to be in our presence. People would come around us like cats to a fireplace.

On occasion, it was also the most miserable I had ever been. Our relationship was not completely without conflict, because we could get ourselves pretty cross-threaded at times. There was so much passion and need that we overidentified with each other despite the fact that we were very different people.

Periodically, we'd have these pretty stark little meltdowns, but we knew—and this was the most important thing—that the relationship was indispensable and that we couldn't live without it. It was a little like living in the tropics. Most of the time, the weather could not be better but on occasion, a big blue storm would erupt out of the sea and tear the shit out of everything.

Therefore, whenever trouble came we never considered the possibility that we would just walk away. That was never an option. Instead we would look at the trouble as though it were a foreign invader that had manifested itself in the action and reaction between our two psyches. We had created a home for it and it had grown up in this home, but we had to drive this demon out of our garden. Doing so required making common cause against it. We couldn't say, "You're doing this and you're doing that . . ." Instead, it was always, "We're doing this. This is what we do here. And at the point where I do this, if you could stop yourself from doing that . . ." We were our own therapy.

We traveled together a lot and went overseas when I had speaking gigs in Spain, but we spent most of our time in New York. I was living there because I still had not delivered my book to Viking. In order to get me to finish it, they put me in an office next to my editor, but that still didn't work. I would go there regularly, but I learned that I could not relieve myself of the tale without someone there to hear it.

Cynthia and I began living together in my apartment at 24 Fifth Avenue, where she also had her office. But then we had to leave. My place was a sublet from a good friend who had spent the summer at his farm in Vermont but now was coming back to reclaim the apartment. It was a terrible moment for us because real estate and romance are very tightly connected in New York. They are deeply bound to each other. You kind of are where you live, and we were panic-stricken because we couldn't seem to find anything.

Then we went to a movie at the Quad Cinema on West Thirteenth Street in Greenwich Village, and there was a note pinned to a tree right outside the theater that described this way-too-good-to-be-true apartment. Cynthia actually laughed at me for calling the guy. "This is a trap of some sort," she said. "I'm amazed you're so gullible."

The apartment was on Twenty-Third Street and Eighth Avenue, and it turned out to be a wonderful place, too good but also true. It had a rose garden and a bedroom that was a conservatory made of glass. As a container for the two of us, it could scarcely have been any nicer. Especially given the fact that we were both exhibitionists. We could lie in bed and see the moon and also absolutely be seen by all our neighbors.

Before I had taken Cynthia to see the Grateful Dead for the first time, the only thing that had ever really mattered to her about music was that her best friend from the time she was about six years old was Diana Krall. This was before Diana had much of a reputation, but we would go to every one of her shows and find ourselves in the cocktail lounge at the Ritz-Carlton. Cynthia was Diana's most devoted fan and best friend and was practically her manager at the time. After Diana married Elvis Costello, she bought a really beautiful piece of property right next door to Cynthia's parents on Vancouver Island and that is where they live now.

Because of my relationship with John Kennedy, Jr., and Cynthia's affection for him and Daryl Hannah—his girlfriend at the time—the four of us became like a team searching for adventures in New York.

After graduating from Brown, John had spent a couple of years working for the city in their Office of Business Development before becoming the head of a nonprofit dedicated to helping the working poor. He'd earned a law degree from NYU, finally managed to pass the bar exam on his third attempt, and begun working as a prosecutor in the white-collar crime unit of the Manhattan district attorney's office. He had also done some acting but had not yet begun his next career as the publisher of *George* magazine.

John had known Daryl Hannah ever since their families had vacationed together on St. Martin in the early 1980s, but they had started dating only after he ran into her at his aunt Lee Radziwill's wedding to director Herb Ross in 1988. Daryl was then just coming out of what I gather had been a fairly calamitous relationship with Jackson Browne, and for a while John was seeing other women as well, but once he and Daryl became a couple, it was definitely what I guess you might call headline news; they were featured on the cover of *People* magazine.

Although Daryl is mildly autistic, she had a great way of deemphasizing it. But it was there all the same and made her seem like she was permanently twelve years old. Right down to the minor details, Daryl was the one who had come up with the plot and treatment for the movie *Big*. Although she wasn't in it because the whole thing got taken away from her, *Big* described what it was like to be her.

John himself was not particularly a dope smoker, but he did like psychedelics and the four of us tripped together on acid. Cynthia and

I also took MDMA with John and Daryl, and that was interesting. Three really good-looking people on ecstasy and me. I was like, "What is wrong with this picture? Like, how did I get into this group? I get the other three but what about this ugly fuck over here in the corner?"

What I didn't know back then but learned much later was that John was also in love with Cynthia. Was I in love with Daryl Hannah? I know my limits, and she was far beyond them. Although I spent a hell of a lot of time around her, Daryl had so many trust issues. I am not an untrustworthy person at all, but for some reason people often feel that I might be, especially if they are not terribly sophisticated. And so I think she had a hard time really trusting me.

It was not out of the question that Cynthia would have responded to John's interest in her. I mean, this was John Kennedy, Jr. Nobody ever spent any time around the guy without falling in love with him. Cynthia was very, very fond of John, but we never discussed this. The way things turned out, it didn't matter one way or the other.

THIRTY-SEVEN

LOSING HER

By this point, Cynthia and I had realized we had become mutually indispensable. Neither one of us could imagine life without the other. However, Cynthia was filled with forebodings and premonitions and had constant nightmares about my impending doom.

These were not entirely ill founded, because *Wired* magazine had asked me to go to Sarajevo during the Serbo-Croatian war at the height of the shelling. They wanted me to write about the relationship between information and war and the way in which the mass media had created a hallucination that was destroying the ability of each side to see the other's humanity. Of course I'd accepted the assignment and had already been issued my flak jacket and helmet by the United Nations.

Cynthia was absolutely convinced I was going to get killed over there. I didn't believe it. I felt that despite there being a lot of bullets addressed to whom it might concern, none of them had my name on them. I offered her repeated assurances, but they were not particularly comforting to her.

In April 1994, shortly before I was to leave on the assignment, I went out to Los Angeles to give a speech and was staying with Daryl. Tim Leary had gotten tickets and backstage passes for John, Daryl, Cynthia, and me to go with him to a Pink Floyd concert at the Rose Bowl, but John called and said he couldn't come because his mother, who was suffering from non-Hodgkin's lymphoma, had suddenly taken a turn for the worse.

Cynthia was supposed to fly out with John but instead came by herself. Daryl was so angry that John didn't come that she decided to spend the day with her horses in Santa Barbara. Both Cynthia and I had been suffering from one of those persistent flu viruses that can hang on for weeks at a time. Whenever we thought we were getting better, it would grab us again.

That afternoon, Cynthia and I went over to Tim Leary's house, and death was on everything. It was the weirdest thing because Tim wasn't even sick yet but looked like he was dying. I never saw him look that sick again until he actually died.

Aileen Getty was living there at the time and she claimed to be dying of AIDS. Bow the dog had gone blind, and he looked like he was dying. The only person who really looked alive that day was Cynthia. At one point, we were sitting out in the garden together and a black cat that Barbara had left behind came out of the foliage. Cynthia jumped up and screamed.

I said, "Why did you do that?" And she said, "There's something about that cat." I said, "Surely, you're not superstitious?" And she said, "I'm superstitious about that cat. That cat means no good."

Later that afternoon, Cynthia went into Tim's office. He looked truly moribund, and so she put her hands on his head and started to stroke his temples, and it was as if a strange transfer of life took place between them. I really don't know how else to describe it.

The huge 1994 Northridge earthquake had significantly rearranged the traffic infrastructure between Beverly Hills and Pasadena. As a result, we had to wade through three and a half hours of traffic to get to the Rose Bowl. By the time we got there, the will call window was closed. Tim and Aileen decided they didn't want to deal with it and left.

However, while Cynthia and I were sitting together in our car for three and a half hours along with ninety thousand other concertgoers, we got to talking about the future, something we had agreed not to think about. We felt the best way to create a good future was to maintain a well-wrought present. Up to that point, Cynthia had been adamantly opposed to having children, but she suddenly said, "I think you and I should have children. And if we're going to do that, I would love to start soon so we should be married. How do you feel about that?"

Even though I was not yet divorced from Elaine, I said, "That's all right." On some profound level, it seemed that we had been married ever since we had met.

We used the rest of our time in the car to plot out the next couple of years. We would move to San Francisco in September and buy a house. She would set up her new practice there over the winter. We would get married in the spring and then start having babies shortly thereafter.

Our passage into the concert was no easy deal. We had to buy scalper's tickets at a prodigious price, and the seating left a lot to be desired. But nevertheless, Cynthia danced like a dust devil. It was a moment of unadulterated delight.

Once the show was over we had to find our car, which we had parked on a golf course next to the Rose Bowl. Because it was ad hoc parking, there were no markings for area identification and we trudged around the golf course for two hours looking for our car.

Cynthia started to feel the effects of the flu taking hold again. She said, "I feel like I want to crawl out of my own skin." And I said, "Don't do that, darling. Your skin wouldn't look anything like it should without you in it." By the time we got back to Daryl's house, Cynthia was completely exhausted, but she still went running on the beach in Santa Monica the next morning.

Cynthia was going to be thirty years old in two days, and we'd planned a big splashy birthday party for her in New York. We were going to fly back together Sunday afternoon, but I got a phone call from Irwin Winkler, who was producing a movie called *The Net*. It was to be the first popular-culture representation of the Internet, and I wanted every opportunity to put the right spin on the ball.

So I agreed to meet with him that day in Los Angeles, which meant I would have to take the red-eye back to New York that night rather than flying with Cynthia. She wanted to delay her flight to accompany me, but I said, "Look, you've been sick and you've got patients to see tomorrow. Why don't you just take the afternoon flight? And then I'll be home to see you in time for us to make love before you go off to work in the morning."

Those were the days when you could still walk with someone right to the gate at LAX. When we said goodbye to each other there, we enjoyed one of our customarily shameless kisses and she said, "We were made for each other, baby. Nothing can keep us apart." Then she bounded down the Jetway as full of life as anyone I'd ever seen.

After getting on the plane, she took a nap. When the flight attendant tried to wake Cynthia up to tell her to put on her seat belt as they came into JFK, she was dead. The one thing that could have proved her last words false had happened.

I later learned that she had an underlying genetic predisposition that allowed that virus to unweave her heart muscle. When you get the flu, you ache, because a virus is literally disassembling your DNA. It was viral cardiomyopathy. Had it been bacterial, they could have done something about it, but at that stage of the game, probably the only thing that would have saved her would have been an immediate heart transplant.

When I arrived home in the cold gray dawn, Cynthia was not there. There was plenty of evidence indicating her chaotic departure but none that she had returned. I started to call a few friends to see if they had heard anything, and there was a fellow intern from Beth Israel who said that she had received a mysterious phone call at home in the middle of the night from the Jamaica Hospital Medical Center in Queens asking if she knew Cynthia.

She said she did, but they wouldn't tell her what was up. So I immediately called the emergency room there and was told that yes, Cynthia Horner had been there but that she had been moved to Queens General Hospital. I then battled though an incredibly convoluted phone tangle asking if anybody had heard of this case. All the time I was on hold during these phone transfers, Muzak was playing Pachelbel's Canon in D, which set a certain tone.

Finally, I got somebody who said she knew about Cynthia. She then put the phone down and I heard her call out to someone else in the room, "What time did she expire?" And my world went flying. I told her there had to be a mistake, because there was no conceivable way that the woman I was looking for had expired. But no, they had positive ID on her and all that remained was for me to come down and identify the body in the morgue.

I called a mobster patient that Cynthia had, and he drove me out there. As it turned out, her skin didn't look so bad without her in it. But I felt like my own heart had been amputated. I felt like Moses might have if he had been given a year in the Promised Land before being kicked back out into the desert. There is really no way to say this without sounding incredibly sappy, but we were the same soul.

In terms of telling her family about us, Cynthia had been very secretive, which was kind of ironic given the way I felt about secrecy on the Internet. But none of them knew about the two of us. Shortly before she died, Cynthia had gone home for Easter and told her father about what had happened with her and Diego, but no one else in the family knew a thing.

After I determined that it really was Cynthia's body in the morgue, it was incumbent upon me to call her parents. I woke up her mother and said, "You don't know me and you're going to wish you didn't," and then I told her what had happened. Fortunately, her parents were extraordinarily graceful. Her father said that he had never seen her as happy as she had been during the year we had been together. He'd had no idea what to make of it but now understood, and so he exonerated me.

Cynthia's service was held on Friday, April 22, 1994, in a small church in Nanaimo. About 250 people came; she was a real star as far as they were concerned. Nobody knew who I was, but I delivered the only eulogy. I still don't know why the family let me do it.

I began by saying, "I don't know most of you, and I envy the many among you who were graced with Cynthia all her short life. I only knew her a little while. We spent this last glorious year together. It was the best year of my life and, I firmly believe, it was the best year of her life, too. . . .

"I don't know that I believe in the supernatural, but I do believe in miracles and our time together was filled with the events of magical unlikelihood. I also believe that angels, or something like them, sometimes live among us, hidden within our fellow human beings. I'm convinced that such an angel dwelled in Cynthia. I felt this presence often in Cynthia's lightness of being, in her decency, her tolerance, her incredible love. I never heard Cynthia speak ill of anyone, nor did I ever hear anyone speak ill of her. She gave joy and solace to all who met her.

"I feel her angel still, dancing around the spiritual periphery, just beyond the sight of my eyes, narrowed as they are with tears and the glare of ordinary light. Her graceful goodness continues to surround me, if less focused and tangible than before.

"With a care both conscious and reverential, Cynthia and I built a love which I believe inspired most who came near it. . . . We wanted to make our union into a message of hope, and I believe we did, even though we knew that hearts opened so freely can be shattered if something should go wrong. As my heart is shattered now.

"So among the waves of tragedy which have crashed on me with her death is a terror that our message of hope has been changed into a dreadful warning. But I must tell you that had I known in the beginning that I would be here today doing this terrible thing, I would still have loved her as unhesitatingly, because true love is worth any price one is asked to pay.

"The other message we wished to convey was one of faith in the essential goodness and purpose of life. I have always felt that no matter how inscrutable its ways and means, the universe is working perfectly and working according to a greater plan than we can know.

"In the last few days, I have had to battle with the fear that everything is actually just random, that the universe is a howling void of meaningless chaos, indifferent to everything that I value. All hope has at times seemed unjustified to me.

"But groundless hope, like unconditional love, is the only kind worth having. Its true name is faith. As it is a shallow faith which goes untested, so it is that if we can keep our faith through this terrible test, we will emerge with a conviction of enduring strength. And this faith will become Cynthia's greatest gift to us. If we can build with our lives a monument to her light, her gameness, and her love, she will not have died in vain, and her death will become as much a miracle as was her life."

What I said had a big effect on a lot of people. One of the things I discovered, even though I had known this before in some abstract way but hadn't ever really focused on it, was how completely fucked up America is in regard to death and mourning. You don't die in America without losing. You lost your battle with death. And so it's considered to be an act of weakness, which makes it difficult to accept the second most common thing in life.

When my mother was ninety-four years old and had cancer for the third time, she had Mormon relatives coming into her hospital room in Salt Lake City saying, "You can beat this thing, Mim. You're a fighter." Such horseshit. As a consequence, people don't feel they have permission to mourn. Stiff upper lip and they go on. That was not an option for me. I had been hit so hard I had to mourn, and I was doing it completely involuntarily. I had no choice at all.

Even though it was still in the early days of the Internet, what I had written about Cynthia, including my eulogy for her, went viral. My God, I got probably five megabytes of emails from all over the world, most of them saying that they now felt like they had been given permission to mourn and were grateful to me for that. Some of these even came from people who had lost someone years before, and finally understood how they could now feel as bad as they still did. Although this was comforting for me to know, it did nothing to alleviate my grief.

After Cynthia died, I was forced to decide whether the universe was senseless and cruel or actually had a purpose. And I realized the physical world exists so that love can make sense, because without the frame of fear and doubt and suffering, love is effortless and meaningless. I believed that we volunteer our souls to come into the physical world so that we can do battle with fear.

Nonetheless, the pain got so bad for a while that if I stopped moving,

I couldn't stand it. And so I fell into a lifestyle of continuous motion. Over the course of the following year, I flew more than 270,000 miles on just one airline. The stratosphere became my church. Whenever I was up there, I felt like I was closer to her.

During this period, I would suddenly—and surprisingly, even to myself—break into a conflagration of weeping. You could spontaneously combust and cause less consternation than if you're a full-grown man who suddenly bursts into tears while sitting next to some guy in business class on a plane. Knowing I could cry there whenever the urge hit me, I decided to go into rehab.

THIRTY-EIGHT

REHAB

When I went into rehab, I was smoking three packs of Marlboro Lights 100s a day. I was twenty pounds overweight and sleeping three hours a night and had pretty much succeeded in creating jet lag as a poetic art form. I had also started drinking again, which was worrisome because I hadn't been drinking at all during the time I was with Cynthia, but it didn't seem to me like my drinking was really out of control.

I realized I needed to be someplace where I could cry as much as I was compelled to do without freaking out everybody around me. About two weeks after Cynthia died, I went into rehab at St. Helena Hospital in Napa. I chose it because Weir had checked himself in there a couple of days before. In addition, they had offered Cynthia a job once. The second I announced my intention to go there, Weir announced his intention to leave, which I didn't think was a coincidence but I also understood it because of how well I knew Weir.

I stayed at St. Helena for about three weeks. It was a traditional twelve-step program, and I went to a lot of meetings. I was in a group one day when a woman started talking about the reason she had come there. It was because her kitten had died and it had totally unhinged her and she had gone off on a bender. She started to cry. Somebody else started talking about how he had lost his dog and that was the worst thing that had ever happened to him. There was also a really rough longshoreman—whom I had not seen shed a tear the whole time I had been there—and he started talking about a pet duck he'd had that had been killed by dogs, and he started to cry like a baby.

I was sitting there thinking, *This guy is crying about a duck? What about me, guys? I've had a little bit of a loss here myself.* I started to say something about it and then I suddenly realized that what they were all mourning was the only form of unconditional love they had ever been willing to accept. The closest they had ever gotten to it was from a pet, because they could not accept it from a human being, which is something that most people cannot do. And so I had to count myself as having been incredibly lucky to have experienced it with another human being.

THIRTY-NINE

A GOLD RUSH OF THE HEART

Upon my release from rehab in St. Helena, I had conquered my involuntary weeping, but I was still unenthusiastic about being alive. I knew I had to stay alive because of my daughters, but the important thing was to *want* to be alive. In the service of that, I decided to proceed with the plan Cynthia and I had made earlier.

We had decided that upon my return from Sarajevo, we would take a long tour of the north country with my daughters. We were going to attend a Horner family reunion in Alberta and then embark on the Inside Passage by riding the ferries of the Alaska Marine Highway System so we could follow the Chilkoot Trail to the north slope of Alaska. I decided, and Elaine was incredibly brave in allowing me to do this, that I would now take that trip myself with Leah, Anna, and Amelia, who were then twelve, ten, and eight years old.

I went to Pinedale and threw them all into the back of the family Suburban and headed north. We had so many adventures on that trip that it probably merits a book of its own. We experienced such beauty, such peril, and such crushing boredom that by the time we started south from Fairbanks, I wanted to be alive. I did not have to be alive. I *wanted* to be alive because of my daughters, the Barlow-ettes.

The four of us had so many conversations, many of which are still under way, as we bumped across hundreds of miles of scrawny pine tundra. After a while, they even quit asking, "Are we there yet?" Because there was no there there.

Moreover, I made several extraordinary realizations about child-rearing. One of them was based on a phrase I'd once heard that was attributed to Dr. Benjamin Spock: "All children are lawyers." It certainly became clear to me that much of the trouble erupting from the rear of the Suburban was actually an attempt to litigate. What my daughters wanted was rendered judgment from me, the Supreme Court. Like the Supreme Court, I realized I did not have to hear the case. I could simply refuse to hear it. For several days, they thought this was unimaginably cruel, but then the level of attempted litigation decreased dramatically.

The other thing I discovered was the art of cooperating with the enemy. In this case, the enemy was whining. After we had traversed several hundred miles of scrawny pine tundra, I could hear the sub-tones of a whine developing among them. And so I would stop the car and say, "Okay. It is time for a five-minute whine. Everybody out. All of you get out of the car."

We would then all whine about how ugly the countryside was and how long the trip was taking and how stupid we all were to have ever done this in the first place. We rarely needed the whole five minutes. We came back down the Inside Passage as a different familial unit than we'd been going up it.

We stopped at Cynthia's parents' house in Nanaimo and formed such a bond with her mother and father that they said if anything ever happened to Elaine and me, they would be happy to raise the Barlow-ettes.

After taking my daughters back to Pinedale in time for school, I then resumed my life on the road, flying and speaking and speaking and flying.

FORTY

HE'S GONE

In 1984, I had gone to the house on Hepburn Heights Road in San Rafael where Jerry Garcia was living with Rock Scully, who by that point was no longer managing the Dead. They were both using heroin, and although few of us ever visited what was obviously a no-fly zone, I have always been a willful fool on behalf of hesitant angels. So I decided to go up there to see what was going on and spend the afternoon with Garcia, who, as I had expected, was in terrible shape.

He had an Exercycle in the corner of the living room with three-tenths of a mile on it and a deep layer of cobwebs. He had more spent stick matches around him than it would have taken to build a model of Chartres Cathedral. We tried to make small talk. It was so small that you couldn't hear it. This was a dramatic change from the wonderful conversations I'd had with Garcia on many occasions, where we could talk with wild enthusiasm late into the night about any damn thing at all.

Playing conversational basketball with Jerry Garcia was one of the most entertaining sports I had ever engaged in, but there was none of that now. Finally, I blurted out, "You know, sometimes I think I wish you'd just die so we can all mourn you properly and get it out of our system." I will not attempt to describe the look Jerry gave me as he got up, padded sadly down the hall into his bedroom, closed the door, and put a DO NOT DISTURB sign on it.

With Jerry, it always depended on what cycle he was in. I had watched his weather cycles for years to see if he was in the dark or the light. The sun would be coming out and everything was groovy. Then he would be all the way back down in the darkness. You could always see that coming from a long way off.

One of the few times he really got furious with me was after *In the Dark* had gotten really big in 1987. I used to put out a little semi-annual newsletter, and I wrote an article in it about the irony of the anti-materialist Grateful Dead suddenly being incapable of staying anywhere but in a Four Seasons Hotel when they were on the road.

I walked into the studio on Front Street one day, and this was the closest Garcia ever came to wanting to hit me. He was so angry, and he said, "If it isn't the author of the celebrated Barlowgram who thinks he can sit in the seat of judgment." And I said, "It is funny, isn't it?" He said, "Maybe you think it's funny. But I think it's fucking betrayal." I said, "I try to call them as I see them." And he said, "If you want to stay around here, maybe you should call them as they are." And I said, "None so vigorous in their own defense as the justly accused."

Jerry also pointed out just how much money I had been making by writing lyrics for the Grateful Dead. In his eyes, I was biting the hand that was feeding me. My response to this was that I would be biting the hand that was feeding me if I did not tell the truth. That just made it all even worse.

I turned around and walked out, and then I wrote him a long letter about how I wasn't going to be intimidated by him or anyone else in the Grateful Dead who thought they could exercise authority over me. Silence fell on the scene, and nothing went on for a long time. When I saw Jerry again, it was as though none of it had ever happened between us.

The last real interaction I had with him was when the Dead were playing two shows at Giants Stadium in June 1995. As it happened, we were all staying at the Four Seasons Hotel, and I was teaching Weir how to Rollerblade. We had skated through the great neo-fascist marble hallways of the hotel on Rollerblades and as we went out through the front door, we found Jerry standing there in the sunlight.

It was the first time I had seen him in the sunlight in I don't know how long. He was totally white. White as death itself. He was like a Fellini vision, or something out of an Ingmar Bergman film. He radiated this incandescent paleness, and his frailty was overwhelming.

Jerry looked at us and snorted. "If you guys get killed out there, I'm not going to your funeral." I said, "Oh, I don't know. I've been to funerals with you where we were there for less." He said, "But I won't go to yours." And I said, "Jerry, I'll go to yours." He said, "Fine. Do that." And off Weir and I went into the park, where we had a truly psychedelic experience.

Later that summer I was in Australia in August a few days before Jerry died when an interviewer suddenly said to me, "You know Jerry Garcia, right?" And I said, "Yeah." And he said, "What's it like knowing Jerry Garcia?" The question threw me for a loop, and I said, "I don't know. I mean, the guy and his various manifestations have been so thoroughly embedded in every aspect of my life for so long that I don't know what it would be like *not* to know him."

The day before Jerry died, I had just come back from that trip and I was swimming in my mother's pool in Salt Lake City. I was totally toasted from jet lag and floating around like a dead body. Suddenly, I started thinking about Garcia and the Dead in this completely mercenary way. I began thinking I was doing well enough now that even if the Grateful Dead went away, I would be all right financially.

Then I thought, "Why would the Grateful Dead go away?" The answer was that Garcia would die, and for me that became a whole different issue. Never mind the Grateful Dead. It was going to be a drag not to have those wonderful conversations with Garcia that were always like the Inner Galactic Olympics of the Mind. And I realized I hadn't had one of those conversations with him in the past two years, because he had really been down into the heroin thing for that long.

And then at about six o'clock in the morning on August 9, 1995, my mother came in and shook me and said, "Wake up, John Perry. Your life is about to change completely." She told me that Jerry had died. He was fifty-three years old.

I began thinking about something he had said to me back when there were always all these Hells Angels around the Dead. Jerry's voltage was so high that the polarity reversal he generated created a lot of infection and heavy weather around him. He could go from being the very embodiment of enlightened affirmation to the darkest, most death-affirming person I had ever encountered. He knew this about himself as well.

In terms of the Hells Angels, I finally said to Jerry, "You know, being a decent human being is tough enough without constantly surrounding yourself with a lot of people who don't even care whether they are or not." And he said, "You know, you're right about that, but good wouldn't be very much without evil, would it?" Because of the way he'd framed this, it made complete and utter sense to me.

On a good night, what Jerry was always trying to do onstage was become utterly invisible and one with the music and the song and the rest of the universe as well. When Jerry had first started using a synthesizer attachment, he did this guitar solo that sounded just like Miles Davis, as Miles himself had always wanted to play. It was unbelievable, and I came up to Jerry afterward and said, "Man, you could have been a fucking great trumpet player." And he said, "I *am* a fucking great trumpet player."

Jerry could always honor the music in himself, because he saw it as an independent entity. But he was never willing to do that with all the other independent entities within himself. Like the soul that camps out in the body. For Jerry, the body was this thing that had been put on him like an electronic manacle. It was the thing in which he'd been exiled from all the sweetness and the light. For him, it was like being in prison. He always hated his body. He was locked inside it and he treated it accordingly. Just like a prisoner, he put graffiti all over the walls. He broke the toilet. He set the mattress on fire.

It may have been no way to live, but nevertheless, there were many other people who were doing it the exact same way. The other side will always have its way. If you're going to manifest a lot of light, you also have to pay the bill.

Jerry also always had overwhelming personal charisma. Saint Thomas Aquinas and the original Scholastics defined charisma as unwarranted grace. Unearned, undeserved, completely gratuitous grace. So that was yet another burden he had to carry with him, both onstage and off.

Just as I had promised him, I went to Jerry's funeral. It was held at a church in Belvedere in Marin County. Jerry's widow refused to allow Mountain Girl to be there. Some of us thought that was heinous. Indeed, many of us thought that. It was all about who was going to get the money from Jerry's estate, and at one point during the service I turned to Eileen Law and said, "There hasn't been this much intrigue in one room since the Borgias."

Four days after Jerry died, I went to the big memorial gathering held for him in Golden Gate Park. I was standing at the front of the crowd when Bob Barsotti, one of Bill Graham's guys who had worked more Dead shows than I could count, asked me to go up onstage and say something about Jerry.

I told Bob I didn't want to be up there, but he insisted that I say something. So I walked to the microphone and said, "They asked me to come up and speak and I've only got one word to say and the word is *love*." And then I turned around and walked off the stage.

It took me a really long time to finally accept that Jerry was gone. Part of the problem was that I had thought about his departure so many times and said, "It's coming" over and over again to myself that every time I experienced his death in my mind, I developed a little more callus against it.

The callus grew so thick that once Jerry actually died, I could not really experience it because I had developed this incredibly strong defense against it happening. And no matter how hard I tried to strip it away, I could not bring myself to shed a single tear for Jerry Garcia. Not one.

FORTY-ONE

TIMOTHY LEARY'S DEAD

After Tim Leary went public in January 1995 with the news that he had decided to die rather than fight the prostate cancer that was metastasizing rapidly throughout his body, everyone started coming to his house in Los Angeles to party with him. Tim had always had this incredible ability to set up an energy exchange with the field around him, and being surrounded by all these beautiful, joyous young acidheads so reinvigorated him that he began looking like he was in the bloom of health.

One day I said to him, "Tim, if you don't get on with this dying thing, people are going to say this is another one of your media hoaxes." He laughed but it was true, and at that point I think he actually began starving himself to death.

Even at the end, Tim was steady and consistent with the path he had chosen to lead. He realized that the very public way he was staging his death was not just a medicine show with a potent purpose but also the greatest theatrical demonstration he could make to address one of the chief pathologies of American culture. He was going to tame dying, which had disappeared into hospices and emergency rooms and was considered a shameful thing to do. As I have said, to die in America was to be a loser, and it was hard to mourn a loser.

Until the very last moment, Tim was the least spiritual person I had ever known. But when God decides to manifest himself in a human being in some major way, he always chooses someone who is completely undeserving of it in the human sense of the term.

Ram Dass and I were both at the house on the day Tim saw his soul for the first time. I had come to Los Angeles to visit Tim about ten days before he died, and Ram Dass just happened to be there as well. Timmy was pretty reduced, but he was still able to go out to clubs with me at night. We were both down at the Bar Marmont at three in the morning, still charming the ladies.

That day in the house, Tim, Ram Dass, and I were sitting at a round table in the garden. Tim was between us. At one point, he put his head down on the table and went to sleep. Ram Dass and I continued a marvelous metaphysical ramble over his head.

Then Tim woke up, sat up abruptly, and looked back and forth at both of us with something new in his eyes. It actually reminded me of what had happened when my father had been dying and was revived. He'd had exactly that same look on his face when he'd said, "John Perry, are *you* still alive?"

With Tim, it was as if the infinite black hole of anti-Catholic contempt that I had always seen in his eyes had suddenly been filled with spirit. I looked at Ram Dass, and I said, "Did you see that?" And he said, "Yes, I've never seen it before."

This was a really big moment for Tim, because up to this point his whole faith had been in science, and the only immortality he could imagine would be the consequence of some extremely unlikely biological breakthrough that would be achieved in the unimaginable future. Tim had decided a while back that when he died, he would have his head sliced off and cryogenically frozen. This wasn't something you can wait long after death to do, and so the equipment was already there in his house.

In order to make light of the grisly procedures that all this entailed, Tim's people had draped a lot of ghoulish frippery on the equipment. That night, we were sitting around the nitrous tank and Timmy said, "Do you suppose that I *don't* have to cut my head off and freeze it?" And I said, "Of course not. What are they going to do to you if you don't? Kill you? Furthermore, I recommend that you don't, because this great drama you are conducting on domesticating death and restoring it to its proper place in society will be diminished by what the media will do with you having your head frozen. My recommendation is that you skip the whole thing and hope for the best on the other side."

Tim said, "You're right. I don't have to do that, do I?" And I said, "No, you don't." Tim said, "So it really doesn't matter what gets done with my body." And I said, "No, I don't think so."

I think because Tim had actually caught a glimpse of the spirit, he had been given the opportunity to look over the edge and feel some sense of possibility and solace that immortality was there in the old-fashioned way. The next day, when the people from CryoCare, who were an incredible bunch of bastards, came to remove their equipment at Tim's behest, it was clear that some of them regarded me as his murderer.

At one point, Dan Aykroyd, who was a part owner of the House of Blues on Sunset Boulevard, offered Tim and the rest of us the use of the club for an afternoon and part of the evening. To demonstrate solidarity with Tim, who was by then wheelchair bound, we had all rented wheelchairs so the twenty-five of us could also go there on wheels, thereby causing no lack of consternation.

After that wonderful experience, I was driving Tim and two girls back home in my rented Mustang convertible. A song was blasting from the speakers, and both girls stood up in the back seat and began doing this shoop-shoop thing to the music like a pair of prom queens from hell.

The air was like a negligee, and the music was perfect. People were honking their horns in approval. It was one of those great life-affirming moments, and Timmy put up his hand to give me a high five. As I looked at his hand, I saw these flashing lights in the rearview mirror and I thought, "Oh no, here comes Timothy Leary's last bust." Because we were packing. Big-time.

Fully expecting that we'd all be arrested, I pulled over right in front of the Beverly Hills Hotel. This surfer cop with blow-dried hair came over to us from his squad car. Before he had a chance to say anything, I said, "Officer, I know what we were doing was wrong but you see, my friend here is dying and we were just trying to show him a good time."

Tim looked at the cop and nodded with this sheepish smile on his face like, "Yeah, it's true. I've just been caught at dying." Never in his life had the cop had someone admit to him that they were dying. He didn't even know who Tim was. Just an old dying guy. But an honest old dying guy.

The cop said, "I'd be lying if I said that what you guys were doing didn't look like fun. But just because he's dying doesn't mean you girls have to endanger your lives. So sit back down and buckle up your seat belts."

One of the sweetest things that Tim ever said to me was that when he left this world, the last thing he wanted to see was my face, and I continue to regret that I was not there when he died on May 31, 1996. However, I do have a wonderful video of Tim rising up out of the coma, looking around at a room filled with people who loved him, smiling, and saying, "Why not? Why not? Why not?" And then he lay back down and died.

Since then, I have made it my mission to take certain portions of Tim's message and incorporate them into my own life by doing what I can with them. I still feel like it's my job to do the dirty work of being the apostle. In my view, this is important work. It's all about giving permission by making an example of your own life. That gives permission.

It's also extremely complicated because much of what Tim's life consisted of was behavior that I would never want anyone to emulate, least of all me. He was a terrible son, he was a terrible husband, and he was a terrible father. He spread false mythology and propaganda about LSD that to this day I am still working on correcting. And yet, he probably introduced more people to the spiritual dimension than anyone since Jesus Christ.

Someone who didn't know Tim very well who came to his funeral in Los Angeles said to me, "The way you're all going on about this guy, you would have thought he had freed the slaves." And I said, "That's exactly what he did."

FORTY-TWO

KENNEDY-NIXON

On November 23, 1996, I appeared at the annual event held to commemorate the anniversary of JFK's death at the Kennedy School of Government at Harvard. John Jr. had asked me to explain how politics had changed in the computer age as part of a panel called "Presidential Campaigning from 1960 to 1996: From Televised Debates to the Internet and Beyond."

Needless to say, I was definitely an oddity at this gathering. As I sat there waiting for the panel to begin, I could not help but wonder what my father, a true cow-shit-on-his-boots, rock-ribbed-Republican Wyoming politician, would have thought about my presence at this event. If my dad had lived long enough to experience virtual reality, he would have thought that this was where the Kennedys had come from.

Other members of the panel were veteran TV newsman Sander Vanocur, who had been one of the questioners at the Kennedy-Nixon debates; Kiki Moore, a former press secretary for Tipper Gore who was now a commentator on CNN; and Lisa McCormack, the publications and online communications director for the Republican National Committee. In other words, I was the token geek.

The program began with long cuts from the debates, a spectacle I had last watched through my twelve-year-old eyes back in Wyoming. Seeing them again, I realized they had been important not because they had decided the contest for young Senator Kennedy but because they had also fundamentally changed the nature of the office itself.

From that point on, the president of the United States became more a movie star than a leader, more myth than manager, more affect than intellect. After those debates, it was far more important that a presidential candidate did not have a five o'clock shadow than that he offered ideas that could suffer real scrutiny.

Far be it from me to defend the genuinely vile Nixon or to defame the genuinely dashing Kennedy, but I was surprised by the clarity and persuasiveness of what Nixon actually said during those debates. On the other hand, Kennedy said some things that were not very thoughtful, such as his assertion that it was more important for our country to have good missile technology than abundant color televisions.

But his appearance, the visual semiotics of his virtual self, was just as smooth as Nixon's was lumpy. I was looking at the first decisive national instance in which what a politician said meant far less than his ability to look like he really meant it. The most striking realization that came to me as I watched the tapes was that Kennedy was not so much elected president by television as he was elected president of television itself, the strange projection from which most Americans have since derived their map of reality.

Kennedy was also an integral part of the process by which television itself became the president. Ever since then, this medium has defined our national agenda in ways that were often at odds with what might have been dictated by either sense or experience, until what we're left with today is what I like to call Government by Hallucinating Mob.

As I watched all those shiny old black-and-white kinescopes, I felt I was seeing the transformation to this malignant new form take place right before my eyes. During several sequences, it also became clear to me that the most important debater was not Kennedy or Nixon but Sander Vanocur. Like when he sprung it on Nixon that his former boss, President Eisenhower, had said he couldn't think of any policy decision in which Nixon had played a decisive role. It was a lot harder and a far more damaging shot than any taken by Kennedy. Never before had a mere reporter been able to exercise such power in real time before an entire nation.

As the only geek on the panel, I spoke last. While I waited for my turn, I had to listen to all these bland encomiums generally larded upon the Internet by politicos whose only knowledge of it had come from traditional media. At least none of them called it "the Information Superhighway."

They all talked about the Internet as though it were the nineties version of the space program, a wonderful and huge government project that America needed to undertake for reasons that were not entirely clear. However, they acknowledged that it would have a role in upcoming elections, much like the one the first televised presidential debates had played so decisively.

I must have said something fairly interesting when I sat on that panel because two years later, I was invited back to Harvard to become a fellow at the school's Institute of Politics. I spent the spring semester there leading a study group called "Cyberspace vs. Metaspace: Border Conflicts Between the Virtual and the Physical Worlds."

I got to live in the two-room suite in Winthrop House that John F. Kennedy had occupied during his senior year at Harvard. I was smoking quite a lot at the time, even though I wasn't supposed to do so in those rooms. Given my long-standing relationship with John F. Kennedy, Jr., I felt like I was desecrating the place.

The seminars themselves were great. Twice a week for an hour and a half, I would meet with about thirty people from the entire Harvard archipelago—undergraduates as well as students from the law school, the business school, and the Kennedy School of Government. I wanted to expose them all to the founding fathers of the Internet, so I brought in a grab bag of people, including Vint Cerf, Alan Kay, Len Kleinrock, and Acid Phreak.

After having spent eighteen years representing Wyoming in the U.S. Senate, my lifelong friend Alan Simpson was then running Harvard's Institute of Politics. I'd actually had something to do with helping him get the appointment, and the two of us had a fine time there. Nobody has a more obscene mouth than Al Simpson. He literally cannot get through a sentence without using at least one shockingly creative bad word. We would get into these disagreements and write emails back and forth to each other that were just unconscionable.

Both of us had a lot of latitude there, and we would pick the people we wanted to speak at the seminars and then take them to dinner, and it was great. This was the first time the two of us had been able to just hang out together, and I would amble down the hall to his office and put my feet up on his desk and we would sit there talking about Wyoming politics.

Alan Simpson is the only U.S. senator I have ever truly loved. Back when he was running for reelection to the Senate for the first time, he decided to try to shake the hand of every voter in Wyoming. On the day before the election, he found himself at a party in a remote part of the state. After working his way through everyone there, Alan walked up a hill to where a drunk cowboy was leaning against a tree with his hat pulled down low over his face.

Putting out his hand to the cowboy, Alan said, "I'm running for Senate and I'd like your vote." Shaking Alan's hand, the cowboy said, "You got it. Because that sumbitch we got there now is no damn good."

Alan's parents, Milward and Lorna, were contemporaries of my folks, and so Alan himself was always like a member of our family. Al is sixteen years older than me, and our relationship was fraternal, almost like he was an older brother. For many years, I described myself as an Al Simpson Republican, and I would still do so if that meant anything to anybody besides Al Simpson. He was a conservationist, a fiscal conservative, and a social liberal. He wasn't enthusiastic about abortion, but he also recognized how things were.

Al's wife, Ann, is unquestionably one of the most graceful, beautiful, self-contained human beings I have ever known. They just do not come any better than Alan K. Simpson, but Ann has always really been his saving grace. Back when they were arguing about immigration reform in the Senate, Al was the head of the immigration subcommittee. There were like ninety amendments that had to get voted on up or down, and all this had to be done in a single afternoon that wound up going on until about two o'clock in the morning.

It was one of those rare times where the entire goddamn U.S. Senate was in the room together, a spectacle you do not see every day, which is just as well. I was sitting in the gallery with Ann, and after this had all been going on for hours, I turned to her and said, "God, it's a marvel they get anything done." And she said, "It's a grace they don't do more."

I also had a role in talking Al out of running for his fourth term in the Senate. I felt he had reached a nadir while questioning Anita Hill during the hearings to confirm Clarence Thomas to the Supreme Court. Al was not just on the committee, he was also engaged in active nastiness and cruelty to her, and he knew it. He just got caught up in the mob, as one sometimes can.

During the time I was at the Institute of Politics, I actually took Anita Hill out. We had the same speakers bureau and she contacted them and said, "This guy John Perry Barlow seems really interesting. I wonder if you could get us together." This was quite a while after the hearing, and she was then teaching at Brandeis. I don't think she knew about my connection to Al Simpson.

We went on about three dates, and it was pretty casual. She was still somewhat traumatized by what she had gone through, but Anita is a tough cookie and not quite the victim that one might conclude. I tried really hard to get her and Al together, because I felt like they owed each other a conversation. But he was still truly embarrassed about that phase of his political life, and so it never happened.

After he was displaced as the Republican whip by Trent Lott, Al decided that he didn't want to do it anymore. He felt that serving in the Senate for so long had turned him into something he did not want to

FORTY-THREE

TWO FUNERALS

My mother died on July 10, 1999. She was ninety-four, and pretty much died just from being old. About an hour and a half before she passed, she made a dirty joke that just about had me rolled over. We had this guy named David taking care of her who was gay, and he took her into the bathroom. Much to my surprise, even though it took her a very long time, she finally managed to get something done in there.

When she came back out, she said, "I hate having somebody fooling around with my bum." Then she paused and looked at him and said, "But you, David, you love somebody fooling around with your bum."

I was there when she passed, and I had already forgiven her all of her sins a couple of years before. It was the smartest thing I ever did because then they all evaporated. But I had never forgiven her to her face, because I felt she would regard that as a sign of weakness. I don't know how I knew this, but I could see she was about to say the last thing she was ever going to say, and so I looked into her eyes and said, "I forgive you everything." And she said, "Yes. I know." That was all she had left to say and then she passed away.

In those days, I was putting out something I called the Barlow Spam that went out to about 2,500 people all over the planet. I had written up an account of my mother's life and death on it, and John F. Kennedy, Jr., had received it. The reason he was late getting to his plane on Friday, July 16, was that he was writing an exceptionally long email to me, which I did not receive and read until the afternoon following my mother's burial.

John didn't like email. He was dyslexic, and writing made him feel uncomfortable. He thought of himself as less literate than he really was. In the email, John said he was so glad I had been with my mother when she died. He had been with his mother at that moment and knew this would be one of the most important experiences in my life. He also said that now would be a good time for me to come see him so we could reflect on this together.

On the morning of my mother's funeral in Pinedale, which I had intended to be a joyous event to celebrate her life, I got a phone call telling me John's plane had gone missing. I was the one who had taught him how to fly in Wyoming in a Cessna, and in fact I'd had a phone conversation with him about two weeks earlier in which I told him I felt like he knew just enough about flying to be dangerous.

My exact words to him had been, "You are always as chronically late as I am because you are constantly enchanted by whatever is going on in the immediate present. It wouldn't do to set one's watch by either of us. This means you are going to fly yourself into conditions that wouldn't have existed had you left on time. Which means that you will find, as I have, that you are flying on instruments whether you have an instrument rating or not.

"I have just one thing to ask of you. Which is if you lose sight of the horizon, don't look for it. Just put your eyes on the instruments and believe them. Pay no attention to what may seem to be going on outside the aircraft."

But when John flew into the vicinity of Martha's Vineyard an hour later than he had planned, he lost sight of the horizon due to a well-known ocean effect that I had encountered many times while flying back east. And he did exactly the wrong thing.

My first desire upon hearing what had happened was to believe that John and his wife, Carolyn, had staged a complete disappearance so they could join their own special witness protection program, get plastic surgery, and have a life like other people. It was an extraordinary fantasy. I wanted Carolyn to have a better life than she did. John had been exposed to the media all along, and so he was far more accustomed to dealing with it than she was.

On September 21, 1996, I had attended John and Carolyn's wedding on Cumberland Island, a former enclave for the Carnegies and the Rockefellers located about seven miles off the Georgia coast. To keep the media from overwhelming the event, the whole thing was kept hush-hush, and all the guests were instructed not to even talk about it on their cellphones. John and Carolyn had done blood tests and signed their marriage licenses on separate private plane flights before the ceremony.

Everyone who had been invited to the wedding stayed in a lovely inn that had once been part of the Carnegie compound, and John and Carolyn were married in the First African Baptist Church on the northern end of the island in a community that had been settled by former slaves. The entire event was beautiful and incredibly moving, and I was truly honored to have been there. John had attended my wedding to Elaine, and if I had ever been given the opportunity to marry Cynthia, he would have been there as well.

My initial reaction to John's death was that it was a lot like losing a younger brother, but over the course of the years we had known each other we'd had a bunch of different relationships. What had begun as kind of a father-son connection had become two guys hanging out. Then John began to be like a father to me, because he was the one person I would turn to when I needed insight on how to manage something gracefully on an emotional level. Both of us knew a lot about death, and he had totally been there for me after Cynthia died.

Not many people knew what a truly remarkable human being John was, and how successful he was in what he was really trying to do. He set out to be a good man. That was his central goal. When John was a junior at Brown, he called me one night and said, "You know, this is going to sound incredibly arrogant, but it would be a cakewalk for me to be a great man. I'm completely set up. Everyone expects me to be a great man. I even have a lot of the skills and tools.

"The thing is, I've been reading the biographies of great men, and it seems like all of them, my father included, were shitheads when they got home. Even Gandhi beat his wife. What I think would be a much more interesting and challenging ambition for me would be to set out to become a good man—to define what that is, and become that. Not many people would know, but I would have the satisfaction of knowing."

In 1993, about seven months after John had saved the life of one of his friends by rescuing him from the water after his kayak capsized, the two of us went to see Prince perform at Radio City Music Hall. We were both tripping, and Prince was going off and the place was full of all these bridge and tunnel people who were swaying in their seats like kelp in a mild swell.

Nobody was dancing, and John turned to me and said, "I bet if you and I got up and started to dance, everybody would." And I said, "I think that's possibly true, but there's also a good chance if we do get up to dance, there will be a feeding frenzy directed at you." He said, "That's a risk I'll take." So we got up and started to dance and then everybody got up and started dancing. Nobody even recognized him.

The last time I saw John alive was at a dinner party held by this foundation he and Paul Newman had created to give awards to corporations that had made significant differences in their communities, and for their workers. John thought if he put me right across the table from him in this slot between Puff Daddy and Alfonse D'Amato, the Republican senator from Long Island, he would get a chance to see me dig Puff Daddy and go right on hating Alfonse D'Amato.

I hadn't been in my seat for more than two minutes before I knew I didn't want to have much conversation at all with Puff Daddy, while Alfonse D'Amato and I immediately tried to figure out ways to make each other laugh even harder.

It was a round table, and John kept looking slyly back and forth at us. At one point, D'Amato said, "You know what we gotta do?" I said,

"What?" And he said, "We gotta get your friend there to run for may-ah of New Yawk on the Republican ticket." I said, "It doesn't strike me as out of the question." When I told John about it, he was amused, but back then the Republicans had not yet turned themselves into the nightmare they have since become.

Some people do not seem destined to get old. John was definitely one of them. He was truly a sporting lad; if he had lived, I think he would have come up with all manner of ways to crank the system. He really did love New York, and the idea of him becoming mayor would not have been out of the question.

FORTY-FOUR

BRAZIL

Gilberto Gil, who had just become the minister of culture in Brazil, had read my essay "The Economy of Ideas." Without informing me, he translated it into Portuguese. He felt it contained a vision of what needed to happen in order to return the ownership of Brazil's genetic code—namely its music—from the clutches of Hollywood assholes who then controlled nearly all the copyrights.

As it turned out, Gil and I had a mutual friend who emailed me one day and asked if I would like to meet the minister of culture of Brazil. Both Gil and I were going to be speaking at Midem in Cannes in January 2004, and my friend asked if I would mind getting together with him there.

Midem, an acronym for Marché International du Disque et de l'Edition Musicale, is a massive music-business trade show attended by hundreds of lawyers, publishers, agents, managers, and artists. They had invited me only so the lawyers could take shots at my position about the use of music copyrights on the Internet.

I had always liked people taking shots at me, so I went. I was sitting in the bar of the Hotel Martinez surrounded by some of the most loathsome human beings imaginable, the European music industry. I was saving a seat for Gil, and I had to keep fending off people who wanted to take it by saying, "Sorry. I'm saving that for the minister of culture of Brazil."

I looked around for what I imagined the minister of culture of Brazil would look like, expecting some gray fellow with a couple of minders. But then I saw a guy with three-inch dreads wearing a dashiki. I immediately knew this was the most interesting guy in the room, and he was somebody I really wanted to talk to.

However, when he made a beeline for my reserved seat, I said, "I'm sorry. I'm saving that seat for the minister of culture of Brazil." And he said, "I am him."

We started talking, and I was amazed by Gil on every level. The two of us hit it off right from the start. We talked and talked, and he was quite concerned about the nature of the future of the Internet in his country; it was then still in its infancy in Brazil. Eventually, we cooked up a plot that would allow us to seize the opportunity to take a major country's policy on intellectual property and give it a hard turn in the direction of sense. Our original goal was to make Brazilian music available online so it could be remixed and shared with others.

Google had just come up with a social networking system that was a lot like what Facebook eventually became, and it might well have been. It was called Orkut, which was the first name of the guy who had created it for them. They wanted to keep the network from growing too fast right off the bat, so they only gave out a hundred free invitation rights each to a bunch of digital notables. I happened to be one of them.

By then, I had already claimed that Brazil was about to become an important part of the Internet because it was the most networked nation I had ever seen in terms of everybody's connection to everybody else. The entire country was one vast horizontal matrix of friends and relatives and enemies. Brazil was also willing to overturn the copyright restrictions that were being imposed on the Internet. It was absolutely the test tube I had been looking for. So I took all one hundred of my invitations and gave them to Brazilians.

Not long after our meeting in Cannes, I made my first trip to Brazil to join Gil and Jack Lang, who had been the minister of culture in France, on a triumphal cultural tour. The tour coincided with carnival, and the three of us went around Brazil together to various carnival events in Rio, São Paulo, and Recife. Brazil itself was so completely like America in many ways that it was weird. It was also totally unlike America in that its people were completely self-effacing. There was a little bit of an apology in every sentence that everyone said.

People were puzzled by my presence on the tour. At one point, somebody said to Gil, "We understand you and Mr. Lang, but Barlow is not a minister of culture. In fact his country doesn't even have one." And Gil said, "Yes they do. It's Mickey Mouse. And the reason we have a minister of culture is to keep theirs from taking ours over."

Most of the people I met in Brazil had not yet had the opportunity to use digital technology. The Brazilian government had very stupidly thought they were going to develop their own indigenous computer industry and had put tariffs on everything digital coming into the country. They were way behind America, but Gil and I managed to change that.

After that first trip, I returned to Brazil repeatedly. I helped put on a conference there with Gil and Larry Lessig, whom I had met while spending a year as a founding fellow at the Berkman Center for Internet and Society at Harvard in 1999. Two years later, Larry had helped found Creative Commons, a nonprofit organization dedicated to distributing free licenses to intellectual property based on existing copyrights. Larry's focus at the conference was to explain how people could start embedding Creative Commons licenses into Brazilian law.

I also worked with Gil and some of his colleagues in setting up *centro culturales* in favelas around Brazil. These were spaces where young people could gather and learn how to create music and art with the computers we had given them. We also showed them how to do opensource code, which helped produce a Brazilian hacker culture. Soon they were making their own *conto culturales*.

Previously, there had always been grown-ups in charge who would not allow the kids to touch the machines except under supervision, so they could learn only how to become office slaves by using Excel or Word. We made it so anyone could come and learn how to work on their graffiti licks. There are now thousands of these *conto culturales* all over Brazil without any support from the government.

Within two or three months, the Orkut social network became 65 to 70 percent Brazilian, which really limited it. Although this proved my point beautifully, it certainly didn't serve Google's purposes very well. Despite the fact that Google shut it down worldwide in 2014, Orkut is still maintained in Brazil because it has remained so popular there.

As is generally the case when big changes take place, there was a reaction. Gil and I got a lot done, but much of it was undone by both internal and external forces. Still, there is more copyright freedom in Brazil now than in America, as well as far more awareness of Creative Commons.

FORTY-FIVE

THE PURE WATER PROJECT

In 2007, I had back surgery to repair a spondylolisthesis that had caused my spine to become unmoored from my sacrum and created endless pain. The condition had been caused by some bad surgery I'd had at Stanford some years before that had reduced my life to five-minute intervals. If I could just make it through this five minutes, then I thought that I could probably make it through the next five.

Based on the butchery that had already been performed on me, I was wary about having more back surgery. It took me a long time to conclude that it was just going to have to be repaired. When I met with my surgeon, Dr. Sig Berven, he looked at my back and said, "This is a very severe situation. Repairing it would mean a non-zero chance of fatality." And I said, "There is a non-zero chance of fatality when I jaywalk." He said, "Oh, it's a much higher number than that."

I asked him what would happen if I didn't get the surgery. He looked at me clear and hard and said, "Eventually, your spine will fall through your asshole." I said, "Then let's schedule surgery."

The surgery was long and scary, but it worked. Shortly afterward, I sent out a Barlow Spam with pictures of the upright and glowing new me, and among the responses I got was one from Alan Alda, who said, "For years, I have been watching you curl in your pain like a drying fruit. Now you seem full of juice. That must be intimidating."

In fact, he had nailed it. It was amazingly intimidating. Suddenly, I had a future that was longer than five minutes. In fact, I probably had enough time left for yet another reincarnation. But to what end? I knew I had secured my legacy as an early guardian of the Internet, but now I wanted to do something completely different. I had no idea what that would be.

I kept thinking about what Mardy Murie had said to me one day. Mardy was regarded as the "grandmother of the conservation movement" and had lived to the age of a hundred and one. She had told me, "Environmentalists can be a pain in the ass. But they make great ancestors." And so I decided that I wanted to be a great ancestor as well.

But what did my descendants really need? After thinking about it for a while, I identified three problems to attack. One of them was that most of the drinking water in the world was dangerous to the children who drank it. Moreover, their mothers were often required to carry it long distances from the source. The number of woman hours spent carrying water in Africa every day was beyond calculation.

I also did not believe that climate change was a myth. I didn't necessarily believe in global warming, but I did believe in global weird-ing because, as a consequence of human activity, the weather was getting more and more violent and unpredictable. Something needed to be done about it that would not load additional CO_2 into the atmosphere.

A whip-smart chemist and entrepreneur named Matt Atwood who I had camped with at Burning Man earlier that year took me down to the NASA Ames Research Center at Moffett Field, California, where a charismatic scientist named Jonathan Trent gave us a presentation on something called the OMEGA project, an acronym for Offshore Membrane Enclosures for Growing Algae. After looking at a set of PowerPoint slides, Matt and I could not believe how great this project was. Of course the devil was in the details but we were both convinced we had just seen the future. Now we had to go build it.

The OMEGA project was essentially a system to put raw sewage into large plastic bags floating offshore so algae could clean the water. The resulting biomass could then be converted into a carbon-negative fuel by some means yet to be devised.

We spent about four months negotiating a license for the OMEGA technology, which got resolved only when we realized the lawyers who were negotiating with us didn't actually have a goal: They got paid whether we reached a deal or not. Which was one reason NASA generates thousands of patents every year but only ever licenses a dozen or so.

When we finally succeeded in getting the license, we realized the system didn't work as designed. But Matt discovered that another company called GreenFuel Technologies had already spent about $70 million on related research and development. They had since gone belly-up but still held a key patent on floating bioreactors that gave us the ability to move forward with the project.

We were able to get Edgar Bronfman, Jr.—with whom I used to have public debates over copyrights in the music industry, because he took all that shit personally—to give us enough money to buy Green-Fuel's intellectual property. We acquired all their research and patents for $350,000. Not bad when you consider they had put $70 million into it.

Over the course of the next six years, Matt, Andrew Septimus, our young chief financial officer who had a lot of experience in raising capital, and I assembled a magical crew of geniuses who helped us design and build an industrial-scale model of the first bio transformer that could create pure water, fuel, pure carbon, pure nitrogen, and pure phosphorous from sewage.

The total cost was around $19 million; we got the money from the IHI Corporation, the oldest heavy industry company in Japan, which had been started by samurai upon the arrival of Commodore Perry in Tokyo Bay in 1853. Even though IHI had six or seven different biofuel start-ups they were looking at in America, they got more and more interested in what we wanted to do.

From its samurai beginnings, IHI had developed a Bushido-based culture that was not exactly a perfect fit for wild lads like us. Matt and

I walked into our first meeting with IHI in New York wearing jeans. Sitting across the table from us were about eight absolutely immaculate Japanese salarymen in suits. Matt and I suddenly realized we had better step it up a notch if we really wanted to be in business with them, and we then spent the next nine months undergoing the most penetrating due diligence process since the Spanish Inquisition.

We called our company Algae Systems, a name I was always opposed to because at the time everyone and their idiot nephew had an algae project. What was special about our project was the attempt to take raw sewage and convert it into fresh water, fuel, and soil stabilizer.

We set up a working industrial plant in Daphne, Alabama, that proved itself by creating pure water as well as a light crude oil that was indistinguishable from the stuff that comes out of the ground. As we proceeded, we solved a lot of hard problems through simple resourcefulness, such as sterilizing sewage at low cost without making it uninhabitable for the algae we were going to inject into it. We also created what I believe remains the world's largest hydrothermal liquefaction converter, which can take biomass such as algae or waste water and produce light, sweet crude oil from it in sixty seconds. Within the earth, the same process takes sixty million years.

Our system began processing twenty thousand gallons of sewage and producing from it clean water, carbon-negative energy, and biochar that was enriched with nitrogen and phosphorous, thereby making it more attractive to farmers who were reluctant to use simple biochar to renew soil.

Everything was working according to plan, but then our champion at IHI was suddenly forced to relocate back to Japan and the new overseers demanded instant profits, which had never been the plan. We spent the better part of the year going back and forth with IHI and then desperately started looking elsewhere for funding to enable us to continue the project, but people laughed out loud at us because up to that point investments in biofuel had been uniformly unsuccessful. All the investors we approached had no real stomach for doing anything that required starting and running a business as opposed to simply selling an idea for a lot of money.

In 2015, IHI informed us they were not going to continue funding the company, and we were forced to shut down the plant and fire the entire staff. In return for cleaning up the site in Alabama, we were, however, able to persude IHI to let us keep our rights to the project.

To this point in time, there have been more days than I can count when I thought the project was dead. No matter how hard we tried, Matt and I could not find the money to turn it around, which was not all that surprising because, for one thing, our company name had the word *algae* in it. No way in hell would I ever invest in something with that name. And while what we were doing also sounded much too good to be true, it wasn't.

I have worked tirelessly on this project, and one of things that makes me sad is I think we could have gotten the money by now if I hadn't gotten sick. I still really hope it happens, because while I don't much care about making a fortune, I do think it is important to leave the world with technology that could improve water, sanitation, the delivery of carbon-negative fuel, and soil stabilization.

I always like to have a mission in life and feel like I am doing something that will allow some significant percentage of my descendants to feel they are leading better lives because of the life I led. Whether or not I would be remembered as the one who had done it was irrelevant. Every year, millions of children still die from drinking toxic water, and I was hoping to use my last go-round to create a system that would produce a lot more water that isn't fatal to drink. Whether this will ever happen, I have no idea. But I am not about to stop trying.

FORTY-SIX

THE FREEDOM OF THE PRESS
FOUNDATION

After WikiLeaks released a trove of U.S. embassy cables to the press in 2010, Joe Lieberman, who was then the chairman of the Senate Homeland Security and Government Affairs Committee, imposed a weird and completely unjustified financial embargo on the organization by pressuring Amazon, PayPal, and all the major credit card companies to drop WikiLeaks from their sites so they could no longer get donations through these convenient channels. I went to the board of the Electronic Frontier Foundation and said, "Hey, we're a nonprofit. Let's create a path through us to help out Julian Assange, because he's doing the stuff that we've always wanted to do."

At that point, EFF was twenty-five years old. More than half the employees were lawyers, and they all felt there was a significant chance that we'd be hauled into court for aiding and abetting Julian Assange. The chief counsel's response to me was, "I'd much rather be defending you than having somebody defend me."

She then said, "Why don't you do it personally?" I said, "What do you mean?" And she said, "You're fearless. You take the hit and we'll defend you. We'll be with you all the way." I said, "I think people may have a lot of respect for me, but if I'm going to set up a merchant banking account and ask people to start plunking hundreds of thousands of dollars into it on my word that it's going through to WikiLeaks—that seems like a bit of a long shot."

I rolled the idea around in my head for a while. Then I thought, if I had some other people join me who were equally gutsy, then it would probably become a lot easier. The first person I called was Daniel Ellsberg. Dan loved the idea and was delighted to join me in cofounding a new foundation that would help get money to WikiLeaks. We then added Trevor Timm, Rainey Reitman, Glenn Greenwald, Laura Poitras, Xeni Jardin, and John Cusack to our board of directors.

Originally, we intended the Freedom of the Press Foundation to be a first-of-its-kind crowd funding mechanism. We copied an astonishingly clever donation method so no one could tell how much money was actually going to WikiLeaks. The person giving the money knew, but it would be extremely hard to trace it because there were three other news organizations who were also beneficiaries.

Not long after we had done this, I was in London with my girlfriend, and we both spent the better part of an afternoon and early evening with Julian Assange in the Frontline Club. It's the kind of place where tweedy intellectuals with leather elbow patches and meerschaum pipes once would have congregated. Although I had never met Julian before, he had apparently known about me since he had been in knee pants, and gave me what I would call a fair modicum of respect. At the time, he was also pitching me to bring in the EFF to help support WikiLeaks by giving him a lot of money (which I, of course, was already inclined to do), and this was definitely another factor in the way he treated me.

Nonetheless, throughout the course of our conversation, Julian kept his gaze fixed directly on my girlfriend. He kept looking at her in the way someone does when he means to form a relationship of some sort. I didn't really mind and, to her great credit, my girlfriend was totally amused by this. Fortunately for both Julian and myself, he was one of those people who fell into a category where I never really asked myself how much I actually respected him personally.

The Freedom of the Press Foundation then began funneling money to WikiLeaks on a fairly regular basis. This went on for months, and my best guess would be that we transferred around $100,000 to him in the first year.

Unlike the way I felt about Julian, it was really swell to find myself working with Ed Snowden, because in my entire life, I have never met a human being whom I have come to respect more when I'm in his digital presence.

I kept in contact with Ed through the Internet, and every sentence we exchanged felt really deep. In 2014, I hosted an event called "A Conversation Across Cyberspace" at the Personal Democracy Forum in an auditorium at NYU. Ed appeared on a huge screen from Moscow before a large and appreciative crowd.

I cherished every moment I spent with Ed because I was so impressed by the clarity of his mind. Listening to Ed Snowden talk about why he had decided to reveal the unbelievable level of completely unwarranted secret surveillance that the U.S. government had been carrying out on its own citizens was like listening to pure spring water running through a mountain brook.

While it is fair to characterize Ed as the Daniel Ellsberg of his generation, my feelings about him don't really have much to do with that. It's more about his incredibly deep understanding of principle, as well as how truly difficult it was for him to do what he did. I think Ed has done more to protect the individual civil liberties of those in America than any other single person. I know Dan Ellsberg would tell you the exact same thing.

Part of what had fired Ed up in the first place was that there were a lot of people within the intelligence agencies who were increasingly comfortable with how stupid and incompetent the nature of America's intelligence gathering system really was.

As usual, it was all just about economics, in the sense that collecting and keeping every last bit of information that found its way into this huge system was a hell of a lot cheaper than trying to refine and filter it. The real question was whether the information was relevant, but determining that would also have been incredibly expensive.

Although there were many people who felt Ed was a dreadful traitor, I thought he was the least traitorous person I had ever met. One of the people who completely disagreed with me about this was General Wesley Clark. After having served as the Supreme Allied Commander for NATO in Europe and retiring from the military as a four-star general, he had won the Oklahoma state Democratic primary for president in 2004 only to then withdraw from the race and endorse John Kerry.

When I met Wesley Clark for the first time at the Burning Man festival in Nevada in 2013, he was sixty-eight years old and having one of the most Technicolor midlife crises I had ever seen. He was there after having left his wife of thirty-six or so years, and had begun keeping company with a really sexy thirty-year-old Mongolian woman who was a veteran Burner, and so they were there together.

At one point, I asked Wesley Clark about Ed Snowden and he said, "I think Ed Snowden has been the greatest traitor in American history since Benedict Arnold." And I said, "General, we can argue all night about whether or not Ed is a traitor, but the fact is that Benedict Arnold himself was absolutely loyal to his king, whom he had never renounced." That shut Clark right up. My point was that by doing what he had done, Ed Snowden had, in fact, been truly loyal to his country.

At the Freedom of the Press Foundation, we have a sizable staff, and among the things we've developed is an open-source software platform called SecureDrop, which makes it possible for any standard journalistic outlet to bring leaks in over the transom and then publish them with an absolute assurance of anonymity. I consider this one of the most important things I have ever done in my life. We are now setting up a whole new layer of civilian communications with the kind of encryption that will make it essentially invisible.

To date, about $1.5 million to $2 million has come into the Freedom of the Press Foundation. The funding is ongoing, and I think this will loom ever larger in public consciousness as we proceed ever deeper into the era of rampant Trumpism.

SecureDrop itself was originally designed by Aaron Swartz and Kevin Poulsen, who called it DeadDrop. The platform was launched as StrongBox by the staff of the *New Yorker* in 2013. We then took it over and have since helped to install it at the Associated Press, the *Guardian*, the *New York Times*, the *New Yorker*, *USA Today*, ProPublica, the *Washington Post*, and about twenty-four other organizations.

What makes all this even more meaningful to me is that in 1996, I spoke to a middle school class at North Shore Country Day School in Winnetka, Illinois. Aaron Swartz was one of the kids in the class, and I still have a very strong memory of him. Even then, Aaron was already the person he would turn out to be.

The two of us didn't interact directly very much that day, but Aaron was inducted posthumously into the Internet Hall of Fame at the same time I was in 2013. His father was there to accept the induction for him, and I said, "Did Aaron ever talk about that encounter he and I had?" And his father said, "His life was different after that." When I spoke to his class that day, Aaron was ten years old.

In 2011, Aaron was arrested on charges of breaking and entering after he connected a computer to the MIT network and downloaded academic journal articles from JSTOR. Federal prosecutors charged him with two counts of wire fraud and eleven violations of the Computer Fraud and Abuse Act. He was facing thirty-five years in jail and a fine of $1 million.

After Aaron declined a plea bargain that would have put him in a federal prison for six months, his lawyer submitted a counteroffer that the prosecution rejected. Two days later, Aaron hanged himself in his Brooklyn apartment. He was twenty-six years old.

FORTY-SEVEN

HELL IN A BUCKET

The last three years of my life have been like a tour of death's driveway. I have nearly died a couple of times and had so many different things wrong with me that it is now hard for me to even remember what they all were.

After I recovered from coding out and being dead for eight minutes, I was taking a handful of pills at home and one of them got stuck in my throat and caused me to gag. I had already swallowed half a glass of water and a bunch of pills, and I aspirated all those pills and all that water and couldn't breathe.

They took me back into the hospital, and I woke up with tubes in my mouth going into my lungs and another tube going down my esophagus. My hands were zip-tied to the bed frame so I wouldn't tear the tubes out, and that was its own special hell.

After they released me, I went back home and started to feel real funky. I couldn't figure out what was wrong because it seemed to be coming at me from everywhere at once. They took me back into the hospital and did an MRI and a CAT scan and discovered my pericardium had filled up so tightly with blood that my heart was being strangled by it. This is called cardiac tamponade and it had been going on for about a day or so, during which time my blood pressure and pulse rate declined so rapidly that I now had acute organ failure at all levels. I was then immediately put on dialysis and a respirator.

My daughter Leah was my medical surrogate, and they said to her, "We don't know whether to go directly into his heart or use a big needle to try to get the blood out. Because we're afraid if we do that, we might hit his heart while it's jigging around." Poor Leah had to decide, and she said, "Let's open it up and see what happens."

They opened me up and found out that yes, my pericardium had filled up with blood. Once they were able to get it all out, my heart went right back to beating normally, and all my organs rapidly began jumping back into the saddle. Nonetheless, major organ failure is really tough to recover from, and I was now actually in much worse shape than I had been after the heart attack.

When I came back home again, I was in a phenomenal amount of pain. I found a Chinese doctor who was willing to prescribe as much pain medication as I needed, and I was also taking ten milligrams of Dilaudid a day. At one point, someone who was looking after me took a quarter of one of those pills for a headache and was totally fucked up for twelve hours. So by then I had obviously already developed an incredible tolerance for the drug.

I became so dehydrated that I had to be admitted to the hospital again. Both my physical and mental health had been declining for weeks. I couldn't make myself eat, and I was sleeping a lot during the day and getting zero exercise. I was never incoherent but you did sometimes have to pack a lunch to get to the end of one of my sentences.

Although it was never my intent to do so, some of those closest to me began wondering if I was trying to end my life through my use of opiates. When I returned to Toad Hall, John Gilmore's house in the Panhandle in San Francisco where I had been living, Dr. Beth Kaplan and others who had been taking care of me began arranging what they called a "powwow."

The purpose of the event was to get me to understand how grave my situation really was and how out of control my drug use had become. The powwow was scheduled for May 12, 2016, with people like Weir and Ramblin' Jack Elliott, with whom I been writing new songs, and Mountain Girl as well, coming to the house to urge me to regain control.

As opposed to an intervention, they wanted to present me with options. The overall plan was for me to cut down on the pain medication and regain enough strength to undergo yet another back surgery followed by a period of regular physical rehabilitation. To make this happen, they wanted me to "pull the wire" and detach myself from all forms of social media, leave the house, and go somewhere else to continue my recovery. I cut the powwow idea off at the pass before it even happened and instead managed to reduce my Dilaudid intake on my own.

During the second week in August, I caught a flu bug that had been going around the house. I went back into the hospital, where they discovered my hematocrit was dangerously low, and that I was not producing any new red blood cells. They put me on an IV, but I then began suffering astonishing stomach pain. They were going to let me go back home until a doctor found I had a gallstone as well as four pseudocysts on my pancreas.

They wanted to remove my gallbladder immediately, but I refused to let them do so because I wanted to get the back surgery done first. The pancreatitis eventually subsided, but the doctors told me it would return in seven to ten weeks because I had not yet passed the gallstone. By then, I had not gotten out of bed in days except to walk to the bathroom once. I was getting progressively weaker while also being given massive doses of Dilaudid for pain.

When I was finally released from the hospital, I was put on a low-fat diet. Having never been much good at following any kind of rules, I began eating all the stuff I love, like corn nuts and cucumber salad. I was then taken right back into the hospital, where different doctors alternately had me eating nothing and then eating as much as I possibly could. I was still in great pain and so I began thinking seriously about whether I should write a book on the truly incompetent nature of most medical care in America.

A month later, I was still in the hospital. I was now suffering from an upper-bowel obstruction and still in a lot of pain. I had been given Narcan to clear my bowels, which also caused me to withdraw from all the pain medication I had been on. I could not take any food by mouth and I was on a triple IV so I could get nutrients and antibiotics and also have my blood taken regularly without having them stick me with needles.

By then, I had spent seven weeks in the hospital, and the concern was that I might not be able to survive one or both of the surgeries I needed. About five days later, one of the top gastrointestinal specialists in the game went in to remove a section of my bowel.

What he found was that, due to the severe pancreatitis from which I had been suffering, my small intestine had been sucked up and twisted in a manner that had choked off all the blood flow. The doctor resected about a six-inch section of my small intestine. He also removed five liters of fluid, decompressed my bowel, and took out my gallbladder.

Because my body had been unable to deal with all this fluid, there was some around my lungs that they went in the next day to remove. Once they finally got that all done, I went into a palatial skilled nursing facility where I spent another month recuperating until I was strong enough to get back up on my feet again.

On October 24, 2016, Bob Weir, Jeff Chimenti, Steve Kimock, Jerry Harrison, Lukas Nelson, Rob Eaton, Michael Kang, Sean Lennon, Les Claypool, and Ramblin' Jack Elliott performed at a benefit for me at the Sweetwater Music Hall in Mill Valley. Although you can only get about three hundred people in there, I signed a bunch of guitars, and a lot of other memorabilia was auctioned off and the show wound up raising about $250,000 for the John Perry Barlow Wellness Trust, which we had set up to help me pay the overwhelming medical bills that someone can pile up only in America.

Although I was not able to attend the event myself, my daughters were there to thank everyone for coming, and I was truly stunned by the way people responded to it. Even my old friend Bob Weir seemed pleased by the way it had all gone down. Although he has never been prone to making such statements, Weir later told me that what he liked best about the night was knowing he could play whatever he wanted and everyone there would be happy to hear it.

For me, the last three years have truly been a piece of especially rough water. Although I did end up celebrating my seventieth birthday in the ICU at UCSF Hospital, I was surrounded by several of my friends as well as Elaine and all of my daughters. Sixteen days later, on October 19, 2017, my daughter Leah gave birth to a daughter named Willah Brave Barlow Dunwody.

Although my first grandchild was born in the afternoon and I was being kept abreast of the entire process by text, Leah herself did not call to tell me the good news until that evening. When I said, "Why didn't you call me sooner, Leah?," her response was, "Uh, we were kind of busy, Dad." Which, when you think about it, does kind of make eminent sense. Thanks to Willah, I have now been given yet another opportunity to become a great ancestor.

The great marvel and incredible irony of what I have been through during the past three years is that I became ill on the twenty-first anniversary of Cynthia's death after having flown back to San Francisco specifically to talk to Gilberto Gil about learning how to accept love. What has happened to me since then has been the most rigorous course in the acceptance of love I can imagine.

Throughout this ordeal, I have come to realize just how much genuine pain I have caused in my friends and family with my own pain. Because I didn't know how to stop that from happening, I had to learn how to accept a brand-new kind of love. And while I have really been trying very hard to do that, it has served to up the ante on what I formerly considered to be the true nature of suffering and its lessons.

My survival has depended on my willingness and ability to accept the love that has been showered on me by my daughters, my friends, and strangers as well. I am now much more capable of receiving love gracefully than I could have ever been before all this happened. And for that, I am profoundly grateful.

LOVE FORGIVES EVERYTHING

On September 12, 2012, I gave a TEDx talk at Cabrillo College in Aptos, California. I decided I was going to try something new and different, and not prepare anything. By then TED talks had become such a big deal that not even the English sonnet has had as much stuff written about it.

I got out there onstage and said, "You're not going to believe this and it has taken some doing to pull this off, but I am before you now without the slightest idea of what I'm going to say." I could hear this sudden sucking in of breath like, "What?" And then it occurred to me that what I could do was sit down like John Cage and let the audience experience eighteen minutes of nothing but silence.

Before I did that, I wanted to give them some context. Taking out my cellphone, I said, "This is kind of a cheap trick but I want you to listen very carefully to this quote by Franz Kafka. 'You need not leave your room. Remain sitting at your table and listen. You need not even listen. Simply wait. You need not even wait. Just learn to become quiet and still and solitary. The world will freely offer itself to you, unmasked. It has no choice. It will roll in ecstasy at your feet.'"

Then I said, "And so what I'm going to do now in the time remaining is grab the first story that comes into my head from all the stories I could tell you." I began talking about the time in my life in 1989 when I was driving back and forth between Wyoming and California maybe twenty times a year. I kept trying to find other ways to cross the Great Divide Basin, and I was exploring one of them on a late September evening.

It was cold and I was driving through Fallon, Nevada, when I saw a guy who looked like hell sitting on the edge of town with a sign that said ANYWHERE BUT HERE. I was thinking, *He probably doesn't mean Eureka, Austin, or Ely. He probably means Salt Lake City, which is about seven hundred miles away, so if I take this fellow on, I'm going to have him with me all night long.*

But I did take him on. He got in the car and looked a lot worse than he had by the road and smelled even worse than that, but a weird feeling of peace came over me and I felt perfectly okay about having him there. We started talking, and it turned out he had been born the day before me in a tough part of Queens, New York. He'd gone off to Vietnam and been shot up and fucked up and had come back home with both a psychological and physical disability but had been more or less making it in New York City.

He'd had a cab driver's license and was actually a good enough saxophone player to play session gigs and had an apartment and a girlfriend and a functional life. Things had been working out for him, but at one point his landlord stopped providing hot water to his apartment.

Since he was still a little bit sideways, he quit paying rent because he thought that if he didn't pay his rent, the landlord would start giving him hot water again. He came home one night and his door had been padlocked three different ways. All his stuff was gone, his girlfriend was nowhere to be found, and both his hack license and saxophone were inside the apartment.

Moreover, the landlord, in a particular fit of ugliness, had informed

Veterans Affairs that he was dead, and so his benefits would no longer be coming and he had no identification. At that moment, he fell through the cracks. All this had happened a couple of years before I'd met him.

I said, "So you're homeless." And he said, "Yeah." And I said, "What are you doing out here?" And he said, "Just because I'm homeless doesn't mean I can't take a vacation." Solid point. He had already started this particular hitchhiking trip in San Francisco and so I said, "Why didn't you just stay in San Francisco?" And he said, "I don't know how to be homeless in San Francisco. I know how to be homeless in New York." It was hard for me to argue with him on that point.

We kept on talking, and I found him to be lucid and interesting. In Austin, Nevada, I stopped for gas. It was one of those *Bagdad Café* gas stations with not much around it but tumbleweeds. I got out of the car and went in to pay for the gas and saw my passenger get out of the car, scribble something on a piece of paper, and put it in the coin return slot of the phone booth down in the corner of the lot.

I took a pass by there and grabbed the piece of paper. It was a little note that said, "Love forgives everything." I got back in the car and drove for a while and then I said, "Why did you put that note in the coin return slot there?" And he said, "I figured somebody would be looking for money and get my note instead." I said, "Yeah, right, man. But what motivated you to write 'Love forgives everything'?" And he said, "Well, it does." I said, "That's a tall bar for it but yeah, I guess so. But this seems like a prayer or something. Do you have a very religious sense of things?"

He said, "Oh, yeah." I said, "So you have a very personal God?" And he said, "Yup." And I said, "If you'll pardon me, the personal God you're serving in this very humble way seems to be treating you like shit. Whereas I am doing okay and I don't have one." And he said, "You know, every soul comes into the world to take a curriculum. Some of us are taking Basket Weaving 101 and some of us are taking Astrophysics 406, and I'm pleased to be taking the harder courses."

The next time you find yourself in trouble, this is something to think about. Because there is this weird notion of karma that is precisely the opposite of that, and I think he was actually closer to its reality than the image we carry.

I didn't think about this a lot until some years later when I fell in love with someone like people only ever do in the movies or operas. I was deliriously, insanely, dangerously in love with this woman for a year until I put her on an airplane in Los Angeles two days before her thirtieth birthday and she died on the way to New York. Suddenly, I felt like I was now taking the harder courses. Much harder courses.

The truth is we come into the world from the other side, which is entirely made of love, where it's all open and could not be more open, into this place of constriction and containment and closure and dogma and terror. We fight with our hearts in the high mountains of the Afghanistan of the soul in order for love to make sense. And we do this by not giving up and by not thinking the worst of ourselves or others, despite the fact that each of us seems to carry around with us for no good reason a terrible inner sense of self-loathing. I think that may be original sin.

Mostly to the extent that we are capable, we do it by learning how to accept love from other people; we win that battle for every soul born and unborn. And that is why we are all here. I think that what it will take to get through this dark time in human history is for us to become focused on allowing ourselves to find ourselves worthy and to make ourselves open to the love that all of us actually deserve.

ACKNOWLEDGMENTS

To the best of my knowledge, a completely true work of nonfiction has never been written before. But now at long last it finally has. And while I'm fairly certain that it is vastly less perfect than it could have been, I owe the fact that *this* even exists to Robert Greenfield, who approached me three years ago to know if I ever wanted to write *that* book. Bob, you did faithfully well, way beyond my expectations, and somehow managed to capture the interstitial meaning of what I had in mind, as well the rhythm in which I wanted it all to be written.

I would also like to thank my legion of practical support troops. Dr. Beth Kaplan, who has saved my life (and continues to do so) far more times than is humanly possible, and the UCSF resident who jumped on my chest. Jerilyn Brandelius, Alden Bevington, John Gilmore, and Johnny Grace: These Strange Angels have been on the front line to help me move this book forward. Kevin Doughten, my editor at Crown Archetype, and Elisabeth Hartley, who steered this project to the finish line. Bobby Weir, without whom there would have been a lot less interesting material with which to make a book. Jane Metcalfe, Katherine

ACKNOWLEDGMENTS

Armor, Lotte Lundell, each of whom has a vision of personal glory stacked within them.

Last, I'd like to thank my family: Elaine, Team Barlow-ettes— Leah, Anna, and Amelia, Elliott Dunwody, and our newest addition, Willah Brave. I love you all so very much.

Beyond this, the list of those who have helped me survive to this point in time—as well as done everything in their power to help me live this wonderful life—is so long that I know I would leave someone out if I tried to thank them all here by name. Since you all know who you are, I just want to express my overwhelming gratitude for your love and never-ending support. Truly, even if this really were a novel about my life, I could not have written it without all of you to populate it.

John Perry Barlow
February 5, 2018

ABOUT THE AUTHOR

On February 7, 2018, John Perry Barlow died in his sleep of natural causes. He was seventy years old.